YOUR HIDDEN GAME

TEN INVISIBLE AGREEMENTS
THAT CAN MAKE OR BREAK YOUR BUSINESS

SHARON RICH

INDIE BOOKS
INTERNATIONAL

No part of this publication may be reproduced or distributed in any form or by any means without the prior permission of the publisher. Requests for permission should be directed to permissions@indiebooksintl.com or mailed to Permissions, Indie Books International, 2424 Vista Way, Suite 316, Oceanside, CA 92054.

Neither the publisher nor the author is engaged in rendering legal or other professional services through this book. If expert assistance is required, the services of appropriate professionals should be sought. The publisher and the author shall have neither liability nor responsibility to any person or entity with respect to any loss or damage caused directly or indirectly by the information in this publication.

ISBN-13: 978-1-947480-09-4
ISBN-10: 1-947480-09-X
Library of Congress Control Number: 2017963608

Designed by Joni McPherson, mcphersongraphics.com

INDIE BOOKS INTERNATIONAL, LLC
2424 VISTA WAY, SUITE 316
OCEANSIDE, CA 92054
www.indiebooksintl.com

DEDICATION

For you, who share my dream that we can
incorporate soul into the business world.

And for my parents, Len and Fran Rich,
who from the day I was born taught me that I could make a difference.

CONTENTS

FOREWORD

Organizations around the world are dealing with common challenges. Technology continues to advance in ways that not only impact operational effectiveness but also bring us up close and personal with our customers. Governments are changing in drastic ways that impact the balance of the world economy, whether referring to the election of Donald Trump in the United States, Brexit in Great Britain, or the continuing instability of Venezuela. And emerging generations—whether gen X, millennials, or gen Z—represent the changing values and needs of future customers.

Increasing uncertainty requires organizations to be more agile—doing more with fewer resources, restructuring repeatedly, and leveraging acquisitions as a standard growth strategy. This, in turn, requires peak responsiveness and progressively higher levels of operational excellence.

Simply put, if you don't adapt quickly, you don't survive.

If you don't continually raise your standards of excellence, you don't survive. If you aren't improving execution to break down silo behavior, effectively and quickly implementing change and developing leadership at every level, you don't survive.

The world is changing too fast to allow yourself to fall behind.

While organizations spend millions of dollars on Lean and Agile process improvement, training programs to develop leaders, and comprehensive assessments to uncover organizational weaknesses, the common breakdowns in execution between leaders and non-leaders alike are rarely identified or addressed. In this book, Sharon Rich calls these the "invisible agreements."

Even organizations that spend considerable time and money to communicate their vision, mission, and values are plagued by ineffective execution, resulting in duplication of effort, wasted resources, and defects due to behaviors and actions that prevent high performance.

How often are you paralyzed by organizational politics, power plays, or egoist leaders building their turf? How many times have you been negatively impacted by victims in your organization who spend more time blaming management, other departments, or team members than they do fixing a problem? How frequently do you work harder because of entitled leaders, who demand that every priority is number one, or entitled employees who quickly disappear when a problem needs special attention that you end up stuck resolving?

These common and persistent setbacks not only prevent organizations from achieving greater levels of success, but also make life at work harder for everyone. Based on my expertise developing accountable organizations since 1986, these dysfunctional behaviors are founded in "invisible agreements" that no one really agreed to—agreements by default, developed over time through unconscious, repetitive behaviors that were cemented into the habits of thought, behavior, and actions—the hidden "disease" of the organization.

As a successful consultant and coach, Sharon guides you through clear processes for surfacing ten different "invisible agreements" and provides you with practical strategies and tools for transforming them into accountable agreements that lead to higher levels of effectiveness and performance.

Sharon shares real-life organizational stories that allow you not only to gain the wisdom of her experience and advice, but also to understand how it really plays out for optimal learning. *Your Hidden Game* is filled with real-world ideas and techniques that I have applied with my clients and within my own organization. I suggest reading this book with an open mind and willingness to alter your mindset about leadership, teamwork, and accountability.

The first agreement, which describes the stories we tell ourselves, is particularly insightful. In the privacy of our own minds, we tell stories that promote our well-being, confidence, and desire to achieve, or stories that tear us down, cause us to hide, or move us to self-doubt.

It's the stories we tell ourselves that cause us to snap at someone in anger or to allow ourselves to be taken advantage of by others. And it's the stories we tell ourselves that prevent us from speaking up in meetings, taking the initiative to resolve a problem, or speaking up on our own behalf.

There is a wonderful tale about a traveler who entered a new town. Wanting to find out about the community, he asked one of the neighbors he came across, "What are people like in this town?"

The neighbor responded with a question: "What were the people like from the town you came from?"

The traveler responded, "The people were awful—always fighting, bickering and cheating each other."

The neighbor quickly answered, "Oh, that is exactly what you will find in this town. I would recommend you keep going to the next town."

About an hour later, another traveler approached the same neighbor asking about the people in the town. The neighbor responded with the same question, referring to the traveler's previous town.

This time, the new traveler said, "The people were great! Every neighbor supported each other. People were kind and generous with each other."

This time, the neighbor responded, "You will love it in this town. The people are exactly the same as in your previous town—supportive, kind, and generous."

The stories we tell ourselves dictate our perception of life and the impact life has on us. I spent years healing unresolved issues that were the basis of my most negative stories, which resulted in the invisible agreements that undermined my progress and success—both at work and at home.

This reminds me of the character Louis Litt on the television series *Suits*—a show about cut-throat attorneys who support people or companies that are down on their luck. Louis is one of the most intelligent attorneys in the legal practice. But, he regularly hears his "inner" conversation telling him a story that causes him to become "unglued" with jealousy, fear, rage, and self-judgment. While a fictional show, this demonstrates that even the brightest people can be telling themselves a story that causes them to act irrationally.

Sharon writes her book with an acknowledgment and understanding of natural human behavior—flaws and positive attributes alike. And she does so with compassion and sensitivity to uphold the dignity of every individual while acknowledging the natural vulnerabilities people face in work and life. She doesn't provide a script or one-size-fits-all strategy. Instead, she honors diverse styles, abilities, and awareness as she provides ways to establish practical agreements for improving relationships, performance, and teamwork.

Ultimately, *Your Hidden Game* provides a clear roadmap built on self-awareness to guide you in developing practical and accountable agreements to transform the hidden games in your organization. Organizations who have implemented Sharon's accountable agreements have improved execution, performance, business results, and morale. This engaging book concludes with a clear opportunity for you to deliberately create your future in a way that breaks you free from past hidden games to achieve a new level of excellence and success.

Mark Samuel, CEO, IMPAQ Corporation

Author of *Creating the Accountable Organization: A Practical Guide to Improve Performance Execution* and *Making Yourself Indispensable: The Power of Personal Accountability*

PART 1

WHY THE INVISIBLE AGREEMENTS MATTER

Spot the Hidden Game
in Your Business

▶ THE NEW RULE ◀
You Can't Win a Hidden Game

t was the career opportunity of a lifetime, or so Meredith* thought. The CEO of a large technology company (let's call them Tech Giant) had selected her from a pool of six highly qualified candidates to step into her first presidential role at Gyraffe, a creative web content developer they had acquired eighteen months earlier. Her job was to integrate the two companies.

In her excitement and focus on landing the position, Meredith had not questioned the CEO's superficial explanations for why the merge was just beginning now, a year-and-a-half after the acquisition. But on day one, she got a big dose of reality when the Gyraffe managers presented her with the list of big-picture institutional changes that Tech Giant senior leadership had been trying to force on them.

"This isn't how we work," the director of research and development said. "We're already losing key people. We can't afford to lose more."

"They've cut our budgets so much," the controller complained, "we can't afford to keep them all anyway."

---

*This story and all stories in this book are true. The names and identifying details of the people and companies have been changed to protect the confidentiality of my clients.

"They're going to ruin our culture," said the director of human resources. "Why did they buy us if they were just going to destroy what made us great?"

This was going to be an even bigger challenge than Meredith had thought. She pushed away the sinking feeling in her stomach and said, "Tell me more." She listened deeply for the next two-and-a-half-hours, only interrupting to ask clarifying questions.

She learned that the two companies had vastly different cultures. Gyraffe was scrappy, entrepreneurial, and creative. The company had been founded on a philosophy of big ideas and supporting the people who executed on them. Gyraffe took frequent calculated risks that often paid off. The founders had carefully selected and developed their people. The team worked hard, but also made fun part of the package.

Meanwhile, Tech Giant was driven by numbers and focused on running lean. Its executives were serious about their work and looked down on those who didn't conform. The senior team had proven that they knew how to grow a business and saw their role as professionalizing and providing adult supervision for their acquisitions. They saw most employees as dispensable and believed in hiring young people, working them hard, paying rock-bottom salaries, and firing the lowest performers each year to keep people on their toes.

Tech Giant had acquired other companies at the same time as Gyraffe, one of which was on the brink of a financial crisis. Since Gyraffe had a history of high performance, Tech Giant had mostly remained hands-off in terms of day-to-day functions. Every once in a while, a senior

Tech Giant VP would become involved in a matter he knew little about and swoop in to make demands or occasionally terminate an employee. This only increased the lack of trust between the organizations.

Gyraffe was doing everything it could to fly under Tech Giant's radar and to keep things as they had always been. This approach had actually worked thus far because Tech Giant couldn't stick with a clear vision for the future. There was no plan and little communication.

From the very beginning of the relationship, Tech Giant and Gyraffe had entered into a set of invisible agreements supported by everyone involved. Although unspoken, the gist of their implicit arrangement was: *We are not part of the same team—and we don't want to be part of the same team.*

They were stuck. And it was costing both sides dearly.

After the managers left her office, Meredith sat back in her chair, took a deep breath, and called me. We had worked together on developing the culture and solving team issues in her prior role as chief operations officer in another tech company.

Together, our first step was to identify and bring together people from both organizations who would be likely to contribute meaningfully to the success of an integrated business. Although the discussion began with deep anger, skepticism, and mistrust in the room, my two-hour visioning process resulted in grudging agreement about what it would look like if the integration were successful. As I helped them to identify and prioritize specific areas for improvement, they became more animated and engaged.

We worked out specific behavior changes that would produce their desired outcomes. We established baseline measurements so they could monitor their progress. By the time the group started collaborating on action plans, they realized that in just a few hours, they had transformed from adversaries into a leadership team.

We set up a format for meetings to keep them on track, a schedule for ongoing coaching support, and a follow-up date to measure forward movement.

Seven months later, when I walked the team through evaluating the changes they had made, they were astonished. There were still some trust issues and plenty of frustration that not everyone had followed through on all their commitments. Yet, upon reviewing all that had been accomplished, they were blown away. Lines of communication were visibly open. Three new collaborative projects were on track. They had launched two new products, and initial numbers were promising. They had reorganized two departments. They had implemented a shared training program. People had stopped jumping ship, and they had successfully made two key hires that were working out well. They'd gotten a new budget approved that was acceptable to all. They'd worked together to address a complicated financial problem successfully. And everyone was taking pride in two recent industry awards based on Gyraffe's work. Their list of wins went on for six big easel pad pages.

All this had been accomplished based on a handful of foundational agreements about what the team was working toward and how they would work together. It was hard to believe that just a few months earlier, they had felt like sworn enemies.

Now, it was abundantly clear that no one had set out to make this an oppositional game. If any of the leadership team members had given it any thought at the beginning, they would never have chosen to play that way in the first place. They had simply become stuck in polarized positions due to circumstances, expectations, and old habits of thinking. Once they differentiated the game they were playing from the game they wanted to play, they didn't have to remain stuck.

And neither do you.

Time for a Game Change

There is a hidden game being played in your business.

It is made up of the unspoken rules, unquestioned assumptions, and the invisible agreements that define how your organization operates. You see, we unconsciously step into patterns of behavior with each other based on our past histories, our old habits, and groupthink. Then we treat these invisible behavioral agreements as hard and fast rules that can neither be questioned nor changed.

Every person has his or her own hidden game. Every organization has its own hidden game.

You know how, in some companies, meetings never start on time? Or how, in some businesses, staff members understand they are not to challenge a manager's point of view? And there are plenty of companies with a shared understanding that people should not identify problems without having a solution ready—which results in people not identifying problems at all. These are just a few of the infinite examples of the hidden game.

To make matters worse, our hidden games are only hidden to us. Our habits and patterns are often obvious to observant outsiders in their interactions with us, as well as to people who are new to our organizations—at least until they come into agreement about that behavior, too. (And of course, while they can clearly see our hidden game, they are blind to their own.)

The hidden game can easily lead to varying degrees of underperformance, breakdowns, conflicts, disengagement, and turnover. People in business continuously define and redefine the unspoken agreements of their hidden games—from global cultural expectations to the minuscule nuances of individual relationships—so seamlessly they don't even know they are doing it.

When you don't know the hidden game exists, it runs you and your business. You aren't playing the game—the game is playing you.

But bring these invisible agreements out on the table, shine a light on them and work out new agreements together, and you'll find yourself playing a new and better game. With the right agreements in place, you'll be more able to think proactively as a team. You can leverage each other's knowledge, skills, tools, time, effort, and ideas. You'll be able to make better decisions more quickly and easily. Things will become possible that weren't even on your radar.

My big message is this: The secret to business success is making your hidden game visible. It's time to change your game.

Agree to succeed. Few companies do.

Game Change Begins with Awareness

Changing your game provides new clarity. Change forces you to flex new muscles and reflect on your situation from a new perspective. As a result, new possibilities appear that never could have existed under the old paradigm. You'll be able to solve sticky problems, help your entire organization get unstuck—and, on a broad level, stop being a victim of circumstance.

As you become aware of the invisible rules your business follows, you'll come to see that most of those rules are not mandatory, but have actually been created by mutual agreements that can (and probably should) be renegotiated.

Start to notice the places where you, or your team, are tolerating practices that are not aligned with the outcomes you want. Talk about this together. Make it safe to identify what isn't working and discuss how things could work better. Look for behavioral relics that, while they may have worked in the past, no longer make sense. Watch for and question unspoken assumptions.

Changing your game means changing the way you see and treat each other. People think and act according to their own sensibilities. Treat people with basic human respect, and they will align their thoughts and actions with the business mission and values. Without that fundamental respect, they are much more likely to undermine your efforts and intentions.

One of the tools that I use to create game change in organizations is FreshBiz[1], a business simulation game that creates profound shifts in awareness about the hidden game, its unspoken rules, and the invisible agreements at work in my clients' businesses. I'll be sharing their stories throughout this book.

In their first experience with the game, the vast majority of players don't read the rules. Under time pressure, they jump into the game based on old assumptions born out of games they have played in the past. As a result, they assume rules that are not actually rules and block themselves from seeing and seizing opportunities.

All this happens in businesses every day.

In almost every game debrief, clients and I talk about the places in the business where they are missing opportunities and wasting precious time because they haven't clearly defined the rules of the game in play.

Imagine a major league baseball team in which each teammate is playing by the rules from his or her own, individual high school experience. Laughable, right? The team would be playing by dozens of different sets of rules and would never become a championship team. What makes champions in any sport is that they play *as a team*. They get in sync around a shared set of rules. They come into agreement about how they will play together. They constantly study changing conditions and work out new ways to play so they can continue to win.

Businesses that intend to be champions must do the same.

---

[1] Read more about FreshBiz in the appendix.

The Biggest Obstacle to a New and Better Game: Your Old Game

One of my favorite parables (attributed to motivational speaker and author Zig Ziglar[2]) is about the lowly flea. Fleas are among the best jumpers on the planet. They jump seven inches, which is over 100 times their height. Scientists put a swarm of fleas into a jar that was only four inches tall and placed the lid on the jar. After a short while, the fleas altered their jump pattern to just short of four inches. When the scientists removed the lid, the fleas continued to jump just short of four inches. The scientists had trained the fleas. Even though the fleas still had the capacity to jump seven inches, they didn't. For the rest of their lives, these fleas jumped just short of four inches. And when these fleas reproduced, their offspring automatically followed their example—for generations. Fleas—so this parable tells us—cannot tell the difference between a real and a perceived limitation.

Humans also have trouble discerning a perceived limitation from a real one, and we have a dangerous habit of passing this limited thinking on to others long after the limitation has been removed, often in cases where the limiting factor never even existed in the first place.

In this way, the game you've been playing—the way you've been perceiving and acting in your business—may be keeping you from seeing new moves and powerful ideas. If you could only see them, new paths and results would become possible.

---

[2] Ziglar, Zig and Al Mayton. *See You at the Top*. Gretna, Louisiana. Pelican Publishing Company, 2012.

To get free of these limiting perceptions, it helps to recognize what they look and sound like:

"Things will get better as soon as we get through this crunch." Be honest. How long have you been saying this? (I am also guilty of this one.)

"The way we do it has always worked in the past." It is no longer the past. If something that worked then still works, you can choose to keep it. But, do so intentionally rather than hanging onto something that no longer works out of complacency. (Besides, have you truly accomplished what you set out to do with past practices?)

"If it ain't broke, don't fix it." This is the perfect recipe for mediocrity. In other words, if something isn't causing us pain, we don't need to improve. Really? In today's world, if you aren't in the process of improving and growing, your competition is going to ensure that you are in the process of ending.

"We do pretty well just as we are." Great. So, you don't want to do better? (See above.)

"We don't need change. We just need to work harder." Studies suggest that employee burnout costs American businesses between $150 billion to $300 billion each year.[3] What does it cost you?

---

[3] Stahl, Ashley. "Here's What Burnout Costs You." *Forbes*. April 16, 2016. https://www.forbes.com/sites/ashleystahl/2016/03/04/heres-what-burnout-costs-you/#2ce14624e054.

"We can't afford (or don't have time) to go through a complicated change process." Do you have the time to keep banging your head against the lid of whatever jar your organization has in place? Can you afford to keep missing the target on your most important objectives?

"............." Actually, your biggest obstacle to playing a better game is silence. Silence equals remaining unconscious—not talking about improving your game at all, allowing ineffective habits to run your business without even looking to see what they are. Failing to examine what you're doing blocks the thinking needed to improve.

New Results Require New Thinking and New Behaviors

You've probably heard the quote attributed to Albert Einstein: "We cannot solve our problems with the same thinking we used when we created them." If we want to get a new level of results, we need to change how we think first.

Look at the most sustainably successful businesses, such as Apple, Zappos, and Amazon, to name just a few. Every one of them has redefined the rules. The people leading these companies understand they need to play their own game in their own way.

Like any winning sports team, winning businesses know that the challenges and teams keep changing. The pace of change keeps increasing. And change is easier, faster, and better than sticking with thinking, actions, and interactions that aren't producing the outcomes they want. They recognize that the only way to be truly nimble is to be in the moment, conscious, and intentional. There is no substitute for working it out and practicing together.

Make Agreements Explicit

The difference between games we play knowingly—and unknowingly—is how clear, inclusive, and explicit our agreements are. The new, open game is all about conscious, shared awareness. It is intentional mold-breaking. It is about clarity, truth-telling, and leveraging each other to produce bigger and bigger results. Coming to a shared agreement about what we are here to do and how we will do it is a game changer.

That's what this book is all about.

Business is a game, played for fantastic stakes, and you're in competition with experts.
If you want to win, you have to learn to be a master of the game.

—Sidney Sheldon

Creating a Culture of Agreement

▶ THE NEW RULE ◀
Agreement is Alignment—Alignment Is Everything

n his classic 1966 book, *The Will to Manage,* former managing director of McKinsey & Company, Marvin Bower, writes, "People in the business are expected to hold and be guided by informal, unwritten guidelines on how people should perform and conduct themselves. Once such a philosophy crystallizes, it becomes a powerful force indeed. When one person tells another 'That's not the way we do things around here,' the advice had better be heeded."[4]

People are tribal. We are hardwired to come into alignment with those around us and to be threatened by those who refuse to align. Without exception, people in organizations come to implicitly share understandings about the behaviors and attitudes within the organization that are acceptable, unacceptable, rewarded, tolerated, and punished. People who don't agree either push to create change or leave. Anyone who remains is tacitly agreeing to live by these unspoken rules, whether they like them or not.

It's practically unheard of for an organization to intentionally create agreements about how people in the organization will think and

---

[4] Bower, Marvin. *The Will to Manage; Corporate Success through Programmed Management.* New York: McGraw-Hill, 1966.

behave, individually and together. Instead, organizations fall into silent assumed agreements. Or, when overt agreements seem necessary, people tend to force them on the organization, producing resentment, conflict, and disengagement—along with noncompliance.

My publisher, Henry DeVries, started Indie Books International as a family-run business in 2014. His wife and four children all play key roles in the business. Henry wanted to keep the business side professional, so he wrote up some house rules that he thought were mutually understood and a slam-dunk to be accepted by all.

A contentious two-hour conversation over dinner shocked them into the awareness that, in fact, everyone did *not* understand the rules in the same way—and that each person had assumed that everyone else was in agreement with his or her own individual version of how things should operate.

When we don't discuss the rules, people will make up their own versions. At worst, this leads to fatal breakdowns; at best, conflicts, loss of time, and a lack of alignment keep organizations from their peak potential performance.

The First Rule of the Hidden Game: We Don't Discuss the Rules of the Game

I recently met with the chief operating officer of a manufacturing company. Each department in the company is siloed from the others. They don't coordinate their decisions or actions. Expenses are increasing, and there is a real threat that revenues will decrease over the coming year. No one on the leadership team discusses these dysfunctional agreements. In effect, there is no leadership team.

Reality will hold them accountable in the coming year. They'll become yet another of the many companies that avoid discussing the game they are in and are blindsided when they lose.

I don't want this to happen in your business.

You can transform your business and the results it produces by playing an open game. Bring your organization into open alignment on a manageable handful of agreements that set businesses up to succeed. I'm talking about the creation of a constitution, of sorts, for your business—a code of conduct, relationship, attitude, and behavior. I want you to have open conversations with the people in your organization about these agreements. I want you to put them in writing and do your best to live by them. This book will be your guide to the following ten business game-changers:

1. **How you will talk about the business.** The way your team talks about your business has a powerful impact on its ability to achieve its purpose and objectives. It's essential that your people are aware of, intentional, authentic, and aligned about the core messages you send, both internally and externally.

2. **How you will make it safe to succeed.** Effective forward movement in business depends upon people's ability to speak up, share ideas, take action, try new things, and even make mistakes. If these actions are too risky, information gets hoarded and withheld, problems are hidden, people

play small, and they shy away from opportunities that could bring big rewards.

3. **What success looks like.** When people in the same organization lack shared clarity about what the organization is trying to accomplish, it pulls the organization's efforts and resources in different directions. Bring everyone in the organization into alignment and the speed with which they accomplish shared goals will be breathtaking.

4. **Where you will put your shared attention.** Without clear priorities, businesses tend to accomplish what is urgent rather than what is important. They are easily pulled off-track by any number of distractions—and team members pull against each other based on differing opinions about what needs to get done. Agreeing on top areas of focus allows businesses to accomplish more in less time and with less drama.

5. **Who does what—and how.** The absence of clarity about how we act and interact leads to confusion and breakdowns. We need role definitions that tell us specifically how each person functions and interacts with people in other roles. Roles connect behaviors to desired outcomes.

6. **How the team will decide and follow through.** The success of any organization depends upon its ability to make decisions effectively, communicate these decisions clearly, implement what was decided upon, and follow-through.

7. **How people will share information and coordinate actions.** In school, it was drilled into most of us to do our own work and keep our eyes on our own papers. As a result, most people have developed deeply ingrained habits of keeping others at a distance. We are unaccustomed to the easy coordination of ideas, information, and action, not only within, but also between departments and functions. In business, coordination is essential for survival. Businesses that figure this out have a stronger competitive edge.

8. **How the organization will respond to problems.** Problems are part of the landscape of business. Performing at a high level in business means identifying and solving problems seamlessly and rapidly, minimizing disruption.

9. **How you will utilize failure.** Failure and success are inextricably intertwined. Every win holds within it multiple failures. The secret to success is to acknowledge this reality and agree on how your organization will approach, learn from, and leverage its setbacks.

10. **How you will hold yourselves accountable.** Accountability is one of the most needed—and most misunderstood—concepts in business. Trying to *make* people accountable creates stress and frustration throughout the organization. The missing understanding is that accountability is an agreement between people, not something imposed from outside.

How to Read This Book

Coming to agreements on all the above may sound like a lot to take on, especially if your organization is already stressed. Yet, taking these on will de-stress and center the organization. Investing the time to create shared agreements will buy you considerably more time in the long run. Still, you don't have to take them on all at once. Choose the agreements that relate to your biggest pain points and start there.

What Agreement Means—and Doesn't Mean

For the purposes of discussion, let's define what I mean by agreement. In this context, I do not mean that everyone must share the same views. I am using "agreement" to describe a state of conscious alignment between people: a unified clarity and acceptance regarding shared purpose, expectations, attitudes, and actions. People can come to this kind of agreement/alignment even when they have doubts or questions about the direction.

Who Am I To Guide You?

Before you embark on this journey, you may be wondering what qualifies me. How did I become aware of the hidden game and the invisible agreements?

Let's begin with a bit of history. In the late 1990s, I was about twenty years into my first career in the Los Angeles advertising world. I had co-owned and led a boutique ad agency that produced award-winning work for clients that included Atari, Columbia Pictures, Tomy Toys, and Cedars-Sinai Medical Center. I had been the creative director for a relatively unknown national agency with seven locations, producing award-winning work for clients that included Apple, Home Shopping Network, and First Interstate Bank. I was between full-time gigs and freelancing around town when I was brought in to provide short-term creative support for a huge telephone account in an agency that was a division of a global advertising giant.

David, the head of the Los Angeles office, was a brilliant young rising star in the global agency who had a big vision for transforming the business. The incumbent creative director, Pat, who had been there for many years and was beloved by the department, had a more laid-back, if-it-ain't-broke-don't-fix-it perspective. They were each pursuing their own directions and sensibilities, giving conflicting input to the teams. Everyone, especially David, was growing more and more frustrated.

After office hours were over one Friday, when everyone had taken off for the weekend, David called Pat into his office, told her that her services were no longer needed, and had security pack her up and escort her from the building.

The first I heard of this was early the next morning, when my creative partner, Jim, and I were summoned to an off-site emergency meeting by David. We were stunned when he told us what he had done—and also surprised, yet flattered, when he asked us to take over as co-creative directors to lead the transformation of the creative work in the agency. We asked for a day to think it over.

By the time I returned home to discuss these developments with my husband, I had received email instructions from the firm's attorney that I was not to say anything about Pat's departure. Jim and I were also prohibited from reaching out to Pat, even though we had each been friendly and collaborative with her for years.

This was a huge challenge for me. I thought everything about this situation was being handled the wrong way. All my warning bells were going off. And yet, I'd been waiting my whole career for an opportunity to be a leader in a major agency. The door had closed for Pat. Not taking the job would not bring her back. The agency needed creative direction. It was either going to be us or someone else. Jim and I agreed to step in. We believed we could have a positive influence on both the people and the product.

You can imagine how the team responded upon arriving at work Monday morning to find Pat missing and her office literally empty. Not even the furniture remained. The creative director's office felt like a crime scene. The team was unnerved, angry, afraid, and demanded to know what had happened.

David called a 10:00 a.m. all-agency meeting to announce that Jim and I would be the new creative leaders. Everyone turned to us for an explanation, but we were forbidden to talk under threat of legal action. We were as transparent as we could be under the circumstances, telling people that we were not allowed to say anything and that we hoped to be able to tell them something soon. We pressed David daily, to no avail.

To make things more complicated, David decided that, although Jim and I would be co-creative directors, he would keep me on as a freelancer. This structure disempowered me as a leader since, as a nonemployee, I could not officially sign off on hires, expenditures, or anything else.

It also meant that I was paid at freelance rates—significantly more than Jim.

David treated me with greater deference and respect, perhaps because the company didn't "own" me. He took my counsel in situations in which he would disregard Jim's. This dynamic created many challenges in the relationship between Jim and me.

David never explained the strategy behind this structure to us. Perhaps he had good intentions. We assumed he was operating from fear that, together, we would become a threat. The story we told ourselves was that by setting us each up to be weakened in different ways, and by creating inequity in our relationship, David would feel less vulnerable to our power in the agency. Whatever his intent, the consequence was that a significant amount of my time and energy was distracted from where it needed to be for effective leadership.

Days turned into weeks, and weeks turned to months. Some of the original team members quit in protest, and we replaced them with talented people we knew and trusted. One of the gifts of this time was the formation of a strong, close-knit creative department, cultivated by surviving this painful transition together. Many team members remain connected and close to this day.

Having placed us in the creative leadership roles satisfied David's sense of responsibility for changing the creative product.

David turned his attention to his business-building silo and left us alone. Each day, suited up and equipped with a thick brown briefcase, David would head out into the world, ostensibly calling on prospective clients. He played it close to the vest, never sharing anything about his business development efforts, never requesting strategic support, never commiserating over defeats.

In our naïveté, we were delighted to have been given free rein. This was just how the agency worked. The roles and cross-functional interactions had been isolated from each other for decades—each department to its own.

Most members of the account team provided inadequate creative briefs to the creative department. In return, creative teams produced ideas that significantly disregarded the account executives' input. On each job, the final output would be negotiated, and we would often end up presenting Frankenstein monsters of consensus. We sold some, and we went back to the drawing board on others.

Once a campaign was produced, that was generally the last we heard of it. If campaigns succeeded or failed in the marketplace, we didn't know. We would occasionally ask and be put off by the account executives. Were they not tracking as they had promised? Were they hiding or postponing bad results in the hope for improvement? We didn't have time to think about it. We just moved on to the next thing. The work was fast and furious. It wasn't unusual for us to work twelve-hour days or more, plus the occasional all-nighter.

As the economy got tighter, the industry became more competitive.

The time frames the account team promised to clients became shorter and shorter. We were moving so fast we would often work from briefs that were nearly blank, with one- to two-hour turnarounds for projects that used to take weeks.

Each department acted in its own interests, not hesitating to throw another under the bus. *Those people* got in our way, no matter which department we were in, and we all felt that we were competing with each other. We could sense that no new business was coming in and felt vulnerable, but not responsible.

There was no safety. Telling the truth about a situation ensured that whatever you wanted to do would get blocked or squashed—and you were also likely to get stabbed in the back.

On one project, we were supposed to present concepts at a meeting. The creative team we were supposedly collaborating with from another office literally refused to give us the location of the meeting. They wanted to ensure their ideas were the winning ones.

Much of our creative energy was wasted figuring out how to protect ourselves, or whom to manipulate to be able to move work forward, or how to ensure that we continued to appear valuable to our colleagues.

Meetings were exercises in frustration, discussing and debating the same issues over and over until they either disappeared or were replaced with new issues.

It was understood that there were certain problems you just didn't raise—certain conversations that were a waste of time. It was better to ask for forgiveness than permission. If something was important, we moved ahead without calling attention to it, knowing that discussion would kill a good idea. We created a series of band-aid solutions, so we were never surprised to be dealing with the same problems over and over again.

Periodically, our clients would consider changing to another agency and force us to compete to retain their business. We won some and lost some. We never learned anything about how to work better together. We had no shared outcomes. Each department had its own focus and its own measures of success. More often than not, these conflicted. We were pitted against each other and saw that as the way of things. This was simply how it was in every agency where we had ever worked. And we had all worked in many agencies.

This was the most painful job of my career.

I was in a leadership role without role clarity. I was responsible for producing results for clients without having access to clients or the response rates. People were pitted against me—and each other—in invisible ways that I could feel but didn't understand. We were living in a web of lies and secrecy in which I participated. We had conflicting priorities and no way to work those out. And to make matters worse, I had brought colleagues who trusted me into this horrid situation.

I knew that we couldn't win under these conditions, and yet I lacked what was needed to change the conditions. Within two years, the agency closed its doors. I was among the last to go.

Here's the thing. I had agreed to this. None of it made any

sense, but I stayed and played according to unspoken agreements, uncountable assumptions, and rules I hated.

Within a few years, I became a management consultant and executive leadership coach because I didn't want anybody else to have to go through this. I realized that too many businesses, led by smart, hardworking people who are doing the best they know how, haven't been prepared to lead effectively.

The Moment That Changed My Life

I set about educating myself. I had completed a couple of years of graduate studies in education and psychology at Antioch University. I began to study privately with a master coach and completed the core and advanced coach training programs at Coach U, the leading global provider of coach training.

I was looking for answers, tools, solutions, and philosophies that might make a difference in other organizations struggling to work together. I attended every meeting, group, and training that I could find to build my knowledge base and toolkit, gathering everything that might be useful to my clients.

One night in early 2008, I walked into a Professional Coaches and Mentors Association (PCMA) meeting. Everyone was engaged in conversation, so I found my way to a round eight-top table and set my things on a vacant chair. In the midst of the networking chatter and movement, a man in a dark suit sat alone at the table, perfectly still, staring into space. I didn't intrude.

Once everyone had taken their seats and the initial business of the meeting had been transacted, the chapter president announced the speaker, Mark Samuel, CEO of IMPAQ Corporation, a global leader in rapid culture change and accountability. The man at my table stood up and proceeded to change my life.

The picture he painted gave me instant clarity about what had gone so horribly wrong at the ad agency: The lack of a shared desired outcome; the inconsistency of our behaviors with the results we wanted; that effective coordination between people depends on agreement; that people need safety to perform as a team; that true accountability had nothing to do with blame and everything to do with agreement and alignment.

Mark had a beautiful way of describing the game that most people don't even see. Right there in front of me, was someone with all the answers I'd been seeking—fully formed, simple, practical, and elegant. At that moment, I knew that Mark was my next teacher.

I did something totally out of character, which I had never done before and have never done since. I approached Mark after the talk and said, "I'm supposed to work with you." This began one of the most important relationships of my life—not only with Mark but also with the entire global team at IMPAQ.

If you related to aspects of my story of corporate frustration, I want to assure you that it is easier than you think to turn that around. In my experience, most people do not want to be part of the toxic behaviors that permeate many workplaces. Too many of us spend time and energy working against each other, and none of us want that. The reason we can't find our way out is that we are trapped in calcified cultures that we don't realize we can change.

Agreement Is the Fuel for Success

Organizations run best on agreement, alignment, and accountability. This is one of the core truths that Mark taught me as he became first my mentor and then my strategic business partner. Mark's deep body of work is at the core of everything I do for my clients. I even changed the name of my company, integrating "powered by IMPAQ" into my logo, to reflect his impact on my work.

People often ask me about my relationship with IMPAQ. Mark and all the IMPAQ consultants around the globe are my strategic partners. We have created and documented our own agreements—and continue to track and evolve them—using the very same process we teach our clients. We embody these principles in every team meeting and every individual conversation in ways that build consistency and trust. We use these agreements in bringing on new team members, in developing our own performance, and in how we respond to mistakes and breakdowns.

We plan together, grow together, support each other, challenge each other, share ideas and, when appropriate, support clients together. I can vouch from this experience that there is nothing like being part of a high-performing, supportive team.

With Mark's blessing, I share these ideas with the intention of improving the world one business at a time. So, with that in mind, allow me to offer my spin and experience on these powerful ideas that have produced predictable, measurable, dramatic, and lasting results for our clients.

The achievement of business outcomes depends on the culture in which people work together to produce results.[5]

—**Mark Samuel**

---

[5] Samuel, Mark. *Creating the Accountable Organization: A Practical Guide to Performance Execution.* Katonah, NY: Xephor Press, 2006. 15.

PART 2

MASTER THESE AGREEMENTS TO WIN THE BUSINESS GROWTH GAME

The First Agreement: How We Will Talk about the Business

▶ THE NEW RULE ◀
ONLY TELL STORIES THAT SUPPORT THE RESULTS YOU WANT

You may have heard about the time President John F. Kennedy visited the NASA space center in 1962. While touring the facility, he stopped to greet a man who was sweeping the floors. He asked the man about his job. The man replied, "Well, Mr. President, I'm helping put a man on the moon."

This is a great example of an intentional business story, in which literally every member of the team, including the janitorial staff, embodied the organization's mission in thinking and behaviors that were aligned with the desired outcome. As a result, they accomplished what had, before that, been unimaginable.

On the other hand, you definitely have *not* heard about the marketing company that told fear-based stories internally about their competitors, acted out a story that they had to steal the competitor's clients to succeed, and got passed over by that very same competitor who went with another partner on a huge, business-transforming project. The company went quietly out of business a few years later.

What Do We Mean by Stories?

World-renowned author and speaker, Byron Kathleen Mitchell, better known as Byron Katie, said, "The world is nothing but my perception of it. I see only through myself. I hear only through the filter of my story."

Fundamentally, stories are the way we interact with and make sense of the world around us. Without the organizing and sharing of ideas and context, we can have no identity, can find no meaning, and can perceive no order. Each of us creates our own experience through our interpretations.

There is what's happening, and then there is our interpretation of what's happening. And these are not the same.

Most of us are unaware that our experiences are our own interpretations of reality and not reality itself. Sometimes the stories we use to interpret what is happening in our lives and work were formed in our youth and have stayed with us. Some of our stories originated with our parents, or our parents' parents, and were passed on to us through their articulation, and acting out, of their own experiences, beliefs, fears, and expectations.

Some stories help us, while others get in our way.

Every business is the manifestation of many stories, the first of which was the story that brought the business into being. Each day businesses continue to exist and grow based on both old and new interpretations, both inside and outside of their walls. These stories create momentum and tell people what the business produces, what problems it solves, how it does its work, who works there, why it is viable, and so on.

When conditions change, the stories change. When the stories change, the business changes. A business is dependent on its stories to survive and to thrive.

The Stories We Tell Are the Core of Our Hidden Game

Our stories dictate how we play in the business world in general, as well as in any specific situation. We can transform our own and others' performance simply by observing and becoming intentional about the stories we tell and believe.

The world's peak performers know this.

Consider how most people you encounter think and feel when things go wrong. Reflect on what you tend to tell yourself when things aren't going your way. Here's six-time NBA champion Michael Jordan's story about that:

> *I've missed more than 9,000 shots in my career. I've lost almost 300 games. Twenty-six times I've been trusted to take the game winning shot and missed. I've failed over and over and over again in my life. And that is why I succeed.*[6]

Stories are tools for creating new realities. Every invention, innovation, and movement, as well as every mistake, crisis, and disaster, were birthed by a complex network of stories. Stories lay the groundwork for what will be.

Our collective stories determine what we see and what we

---

[6] Jordan, Michael (script from 1997 Nike commercial) https://www.cbsnews.com/pictures/celebs-who-went-from-failures-to-success-stories/8/. Accessed September 20, 2017.

miss, what we value and devalue. They influence where we put our focus and what we ignore, how we evaluate, how we decide, what we choose and how we follow through. Stories impact who we hire and how we onboard people—and how we encourage high performance or underperformance—everything that goes into how we play the game.

Stories determine what the people in an organization believe is possible. While what is said today may be based on past interpretations of past experiences, when people talk about what a company is good at or bad at, that story influences what they *will be* good at or bad at in the future. Stories create brand perception internally and externally. Brand perception creates reality.

Negative and limiting stories get in the way of the team's ability to execute. Stories themselves can create challenges and interfere with needed change. Even when stories are founded on external conditions beyond the organization's control, how these stories are managed can be the difference between success and failure.

This is why leaders in any organization who want to take performance to a higher level had best take a good hard look at the stories being told—and the stories *not being told*—about the business.

Business Culture Is Stories in Alignment

According to a 2003 scholarly article in *Management Communication Quarterly*, Enron's demise was ultimately the result of a failure to consistently communicate appropriate values.[7] In the business publication, *The Verge*, a forensic dissection of Blackberry's mobile

---

[7] Seeger, M.W. and R. R. Ulmer. "Explaining Enron: Communication and Responsible Leadership." *Management Communication Quarterly*. (1) 2003. http://www.instituteforpr.org/explaining-enron-communication-and-responsible-leadership/.

failure determined their plummet was caused by internal conservatism and complacency.[8] It's not hard to imagine the stories being told inside of these and other organizations that set them up to fail.

Tony Hsieh, CEO of Zappos, gets the story concept. Every last employee at Zappos is expected to live their corporate story: "Zappos is a customer service company that just happens to sell shoes." This story directs all decisions and every behavior—and took the company from struggling startup in 2000 to its acquisition by Amazon for $1.2 billion in 2009.

Getting team members' stories aligned behind their organization's purpose, services, quality, customer experience, and so on is a priority for most of the standout organizations that have dominated their industries and the mindshare of the marketplace in recent years. Google, Apple, Twitter, Facebook, Southwest Air, Nike, and Disney are just a few. Their stories are so strong and consistent that, if you think for a moment, you'll realize you already know what they are. It takes aligned stories inside an organization to create aligned stories outside.

Unintentional Stories Rarely Work Out

"We humans are hardwired for self-protection. We are built to assume that the rustling in the bushes is always bad news."[9] This astute quote from David Maxfield, co-author of bestseller *Crucial Conversations*, sums up what happens in so many businesses.

Take Sandy, for example. He was an executive in a family-owned

---

[8] Savov, Vlad. "BlackBerry's Success Led to Its Failure." *The Verge*. September 30, 2016. http://www.theverge.com/2016/9/30/13119924/blackberry-failure-success.

[9] Maxfield, David, and Grenny, Joseph. "Culture 2.0: Leveraging Culture for Breakthrough Results." White paper, VitalSmarts. https://www.vitalsmarts.com/resource-center/

business that had been independent for more than 100 years. It had been slow to change and had gotten into financial hot water. The family decided the only way to survive was to sell, and a huge conglomerate had acquired them.

The conglomerate's strategy was to rapidly bring their new acquisition over to their more modern, data-driven approach. On day one, a team from the new parent organization arrived to lay down the new laws, much to the dismay of everyone in the business.

Sandy turned to a colleague and quipped, twisting the name of their acquirer into a new word that suggested carnage. The insult caught on and spread like wildfire amongst the acquired employees.

This story, which implied danger and abuse, created a fierce environment of victimization, noncompliance, and resistance. Can you spot the invisible agreement? It involved passive opposition and victim behavior.

Ultimately, the parent organization deconstructed the business, absorbing the pieces leadership thought would add value to other parts of the organization.

Negative stories are contagious. That's why, left to chance, it's far more likely that people will align behind destructive stories than stories that will create growth. Creating the right stories to grow an organization and the alignment behind these stories takes work. And the work is well worth it.

By the way; not working on your stories is not an option. You can either work on them today and build from the front end or be forced to work on them from the back end when unintended stories take root. The former approach is less expensive, less painful, and more likely to lead to success than the latter.

The Impact of the Stories We Tell

People believe their stories. They own their stories. They think their stories are *The Truth*. They live them out as if nothing else were possible.

Every story we tell spawns other, related stories, which give birth to even more stories. This creates a massive domino effect which can result in big or small thinking, powerful creative or destructive action, constricting or turbocharging creativity, victim or accountable behaviors, and much more.

Our stories set in motion:

- Our desired outcomes, financial and otherwise
- Our roles
- Our decisions
- Our follow-through
- How we treat each other
- How we communicate
- How we identify and solve problems
- How we deal with setbacks
- Our customer service
- The acquisition and retention of talent and clients
- Our impact on others
- Our brand and reputation

The list goes on and on. Stories within and about an organization don't merely impact—they *determine* everything an organization does and what is ultimately possible (or not) for the organization.

Four Common Victim Story Traps That Set up Organizations to Fail

While some stories are unique to an organization, others seem to be universal. Every organization that wants to avoid victim behaviors and create accountability for success needs to watch out for these commonplace culprits.

- **Comparison stories.** As humans, we are hardwired to compare ourselves and our companies to others. Comparison stories can be intensely private and buried so deep we can only hear their whispers. Or for some of us, these stories scream loudly on the surface of everything we do. Regardless, as soon as we believe that we are better or worse, growth and learning tend to stop. Negative judgments become self-fulfilling prophecies. Even flattering versions of comparison stories set us up to stop learning and ultimately fall behind.

- **Blame stories.** Whether focused on others, circumstances, or ourselves, the act of blaming separates us from ownership of a situation and from our ability to take action toward creating the outcomes we want. When things don't go as expected, our best move is to assess, figure out how to respond, take action, and learn. Blame only gets in the way.

- **Fear stories.** People have a self-protective mechanism that helps us spot danger. All too often, this goes into overdrive and causes us to embellish and build on these stories and react from fear rather than empowerment. Growth and forward movement depend on feelings of psychological safety, fearlessness, and belief in ourselves and others. Fear stories insidiously block our ability to grow.

- **Stories based on assumptions.** We humans have the curious tendency to assume knowledge without asking questions to discover the truth—including believing that we know what other people are thinking and what they intend. We are very often wrong in these assumptions, however, and send ourselves, and our organizations, off on expensive wild goose chases. When confronted with the truth of the situation, all too often we will look for evidence to prove our stories were justified. All this does is keep us trapped in victim mindsets and behaviors.

Identify Your Dysfunctional Stories

Awareness that the stories you tell might be impeding your growth is the first step to creating new, success-generating stories. Here are a few places to look for stories that could be getting between you and your desired outcomes:

- Money and compensation
- Time and deadlines
- Resource availability
- What is and isn't possible

- Current clients

- Staff from management's perspective

- Management from staff's perspective

- The competition

- The economy

- Company policies

- Any project that is not going according to plan

- Any person who is underperforming

Three Powerful Mindset Shifts to Agree On

According to Carol Dweck, author of *Mindset: The New Psychology of Success*, "It's about seeing things in a new way. When people... change to a growth mindset, they change from a judge-and-be-judged framework to a learn-and-help-learn framework. Their commitment is to growth, and growth takes plenty of time, effort, and mutual support."[10]

Start to see things in a new way in your organization. Change your frameworks from these disempowering victim stories to growth-inducing accountable ones.

- **Shift 1: From fear to possibility.** Agree to move from a focus on what cannot be done and why to what you can do together and what that might lead to.

- **Shift 2: From judgment to acceptance.** Agree to move on from labels of "good" or "bad" to accepting that "it is what it is"—and figure out what's next. Acceptance doesn't mean allowing something that doesn't work to continue. It does

---

[10] Dweck, Carol S. *Mindset: The New Psychology of Success*. New York: Ballantine Books, 2008.

mean letting go of the story that it should be different than it is right now.

- **Shift 3: From blame to ownership.** Agree to drop finger-pointing in any direction and replace that with a focus on what you need to do next to produce the results you want.

Support each other (agree how you'll do that) in releasing these habits that have been in practice for years and years. Go for improvement, not perfection.

Determine Whether Organizational Stories Are On or Off Track

Dysfunctional stories divert people from their desired paths. They have an insidious way of convincing us they are true, blinding us to their existence and dissuading us from questioning them.

So, question them we must. I like to use Byron Katie's simple four-question plus turn-around approach.[11] First, identify the story that you suspect may be off-track and then ask, and be rigorous in answering literally:

1. Is it true?

2. Can I be absolutely certain it is true?

3. When I attach to this thought (story), how do I respond?

4. Without this thought (story), who am I?

Finally, turn the thought or statement around to its opposite, and look for evidence that may support the *opposite* story being just as true as the original.

---

[11] For more on this approach, visit www.thework.com or read *Loving What Is: Four Questions That Can Change Your Life*. New York: Crown Publishing, 2002, or any of Byron Katie's other excellent books.

How Do We Deal with Stories that Deviate?

For most organizations, when someone is talking in ways that don't comport with what we want, the temptation is to squash them. This is rarely the right answer. Stories show up for a reason. They have important lessons to teach, and they need to be addressed. Attempts to eradicate them will send them underground, where they can fester and grow into much more difficult challenges.

If an unaligned or undesirable message emerges, the first thing to do is listen and be curious. This is true whether it comes from you or somebody else. Be open to seeing the truth, even if not all aspects of what is being said are true. Do not underestimate the power of what underlies the message. Seek to understand the views of the person or people sharing the story. Strive to find common ground regarding shared desired outcomes. Brainstorm solutions. Reframe the story in alignment with desired outcomes and a new direction.

Leaders need to become masters of story. We need to encourage authentic and positive communication. As we hire and onboard people, we need to align them with the desired stories of the organization. We need to develop the skills to understand and redirect chatter that distracts the team and rebuild new stories that align with our mission. We need to sustain productive messages, even in the face of challenging conditions that arise outside of our control.

What You Are Agreeing To

Gossip was the way of things at Natalie's law firm. Natalie and her partner, Bella, talked about each other behind their backs. Everyone talked about the partners' inability to get along amongst themselves, and on particularly bad days, frustrated comments about what was going on in the firm leaked into conversations with clients. One day, a client made a comment to Natalie about hearing there was trouble at the firm and wondering if he needed to move his business elsewhere, and Natalie knew something needed to change immediately. She had recently seen me speak about the power of stories in business and gave me a call.

We got the team together and talked about how the firm needed to be seen by its clients and prospects to be successful. We decided the best stories would connect people with the value the firm provided. We defined an ideal profile to guide all stories about the firm: knowledgeable, constructive, respectful, and authentic. We agreed to continuously flag and evaluate stories they heard from themselves or others about the organization and its people, clients, competitors, vendors, and communities. We agreed that when negative stories surfaced, they would listen and learn. And they would not expect perfection, but instead, would support people in telling consistent stories rather than blaming them for inconsistent ones. We agreed to cultivate new stories by changing behaviors, not just by making up new stories. We put in place a practice of sharing success stories in their meetings and in their social media and marketing efforts.

Three months later, you could feel the difference the minute you walked through the front doors. There was a new buzz about the place.

Success stories were being told in the halls. The gossip hadn't completely stopped, but its character had changed. It was almost all positive.

Either We Tell the Stories, or the Stories Tell Us

Becoming intentional about the stories we tell doesn't mean being robotic, scripted, or inauthentic. Simply agree on some clear guidelines and intentions, so the team is able to know when stories are aligned with desired outcomes—and when they are not.

You can't get everyone on the same page unless they feel safe to have the conversation. That's what we'll talk about next.

Create a Visible Agreement about How You Will Talk about the Business

Agree on how the team will:

- Define and embody stories that create success
- Talk constructively, respectfully, and authentically
- Use language that connects people with the value the organization provides
- Continuously identify and evaluate stories told about the organization and its people, clients, competitors, vendors and communities
- Listen and learn from what is being said
- Strive to align stories for authentic consistency
- Neither force, nor manipulate, nor shut stories down
- Cultivate new stories by changing behaviors
- Not expect perfection

Don't believe everything you think.

—**Byron Katie**

The Second Agreement: How We Will Make It Safe to Succeed

▶ THE NEW RULE ◀
PSYCHOLOGICAL SAFETY IS THE PREREQUISITE FOR SUSTAINABLE SUCCESS

Several years ago, I worked with a manufacturing client. Every week, my excitement grew on the drive there. Why? There was a buzz of energy throughout the place. People congregated in the common areas, sharing ideas and bantering playfully. They were up to something important.

There were plenty of daily conflicts and debates about ideas and directions, yet the team enjoyed the discourse and respected each other's differing opinions. Management listened and provided support. People felt valued. Their work produced over $80 million in revenues for the company that year. And they were proud of the expertise that had led to an unheard-of zero failure rate on their flagship product. (It is normal in manufacturing to expect a percentage of product malfunctions. A failure rate of 2 to 3 percent is considered quite good. Many manufacturers have failure rates that are substantially higher.)

Each week, I drove back to my office feeling grateful for the opportunity to be involved in this culture of purpose and accomplishment. It was obvious that most team members shared this feeling.

One year later, just a few months following a change in senior leadership, the difference was palpable. An inner circle had formed, and those not in it were excluded from meetings and decisions. The common areas were empty and quiet. People now worked and took meetings behind closed doors. Anyone who brought up problems was grilled by the top dogs. As a result, healthy challenge and conflict were things of the past. People kept quiet, even when problems arose. Within eighteen months, their failure rate leaped to over 15 percent, at significant cost to their bottom line, their morale, and their reputation.

What Do We Mean by Psychological Safety?

In her TEDx talk, "Building A Psychologically Safe Workplace," Harvard Business School Professor Amy Edmondson defines psychological safety as: "The belief that one will not be punished or humiliated for speaking up with ideas, questions, concerns or mistakes."[12] Edmondson points out that in the absence of safety, people are "silent when voice is necessary"—all too often with disastrous results. But, she says, not every workplace is like this. There are those special few in which it's not merely okay—but expected—for people to share ideas, point to problems, and contribute openly. These companies know high performance depends on this and they work hard to create cultures that make it safe for people to do so.

---

[12] Edmondson, Amy. "Building a Psychologically Safe Workplace," talk given at TEDxHGSE May 4, 2014. http://www.youtube.com/watch?v=LhoLuui9gX8.

Google is one of these extraordinary workplaces. In 2015, they published a list of the five traits that their most successful teams shared. First on the list: psychological safety.

Companies invest millions of dollars to improve physical safety in the workplace because they can see the high costs their business incurs due to accidents, not only related to worker's comp, but also to losses in productivity, reputation and morale. However, the costs of a lack of *psychological* safety, while less visible, can be far more devastating, affecting everything a business does, including physical safety and threatening its very viability.

Safety and Comfort Are Not the Same

According to Annie Hyman Pratt, CEO of IMPAQ Entrepreneur (and former CEO of The Coffee Bean & Tea Leaf), "When we are working with someone and we want them to take more responsibility, our hardwired reaction is to demand more—to tell them what they are doing wrong. That is the opposite of what is needed because people are already struggling inside; already having a hard time doing the right thing because they are in a challenge. If they could have, they would have. Instead, we have to provide a good amount of support; to increase psychological safety which builds trust and increases performance."

In the work that we do at IMPAQ and IMPAQ Entrepreneur, we show our clients how to create *psychologically safe* environments, as opposed to *comfortable* ones. What's the difference? Think about a time when you have been comfortable. Did you want to change that? Unlikely. We humans are hardwired to avoid discomfort.

Conversely, think about a time when you knew change was needed, but the risk or consequences of getting it wrong were very high. Were you ready to leap forward? Probably not.

In the first case, people are too complacent to move; in the other, too fearful. But in between these two experiences is what Mark Samuel of IMPAQ Corporation calls the Safety Zone of Discomfort (see the diagram below).

In a psychologically safe environment, the experience is one of needing and wanting to grow—recognizing the opportunity to strive for a better place and a higher level of performance. Moving into the new is definitely not comfortable. But when we feel safe to try something new, to know that mistakes are expected and even encouraged, we can step into change and create momentum toward desired outcomes. There is no experience more exciting than this, and no way of being that better supports business growth and success.

Per Pratt, "The more psychological safety you can generate, the more you can request people to get outside of their comfort zones."

How Safety Affects Behavior

A Person Unsafe with Change	A Person Safe with Change
Punishment Zone	Punishment Zone
Safety zone	Safety Zone
Comfort Zone	Comfort Zone

© 2006, Mark Samuel

Psychological Safety = Better Business Results

Safety in business matters—not only in the it's-the-right-thing-to-do sense, but also in the bottom-line, it's-better-for-business sense. In fact, psychological safety is the key influencer for stress levels, employee engagement, productivity, and error rates.

Research by the American Psychological Association, Gallup, Queens School of Business, and others confirms the high costs associated with a lack of safety:

- Workplace stress and disengagement collectively costs American businesses more than 550 million lost workdays, leads to an increase of almost 50 percent in voluntary turnover every year,[13] and costs between $483 billion and $605 billion.[14]

- Costs associated with turnover can be as high as 213 percent of an employee's annual salary[15] and 75 percent of the causes are preventable.[16]

- Health care costs at high-stress organizations are nearly 50 percent greater than in organizations with positive cultures.[13]

- 51 percent of American workers are actively disengaged,[14]

---

[13] Seppala, Emma, and Kim Cameron. "Proof That Positive Work Cultures Are More Productive." Harvard Business Review. May 08, 2017. https://hbr.org/2015/12/proof-that-positive-work-cultures-are-more-productive.

[14] Gallup, Inc. 2017 report "State of the American Workplace." Gallup.com. http://www.gallup.com/reports/199961/state-american-workplace-report-2017.aspx.

[15] Boushey, Heather, and Sarah Jane Glynn. "There Are Significant Business Costs to Replacing Employees." https://www.americanprogress.org/wp-content/uploads/2012/11/CostofTurnover.pdf.

[16] Work Institute "2017 Retention Report—Trends, Reasons & Recommendations." info.workinstitute.com.

and this costs American companies between $450 to $550 billion a year in lost productivity.[17]

- Organizations with low employee engagement have 37 percent higher absenteeism, 18 percent lower productivity, 16 percent lower profitability, 37 percent lower job growth, and 65 percent lower share price over time. [14]

- There is much more research on this topic—this is just a small sampling.

On the other hand, Gallup's 2017 State of the American Workplace report shows companies in the top 25 percent on engagement level have the opposite experience:[14]

- 21 percent greater profitability

- 17 percent greater productivity

- 20 percent higher sales

- 10 percent higher customer ratings

- 40 percent fewer quality defects

- 70 percent fewer employee safety incidents

- 58 percent fewer patient safety incidents

- 41 percent lower absenteeism

- 24 percent lower turnover in high-turnover organizations and 59 percent lower turnover in low-turnover organizations

Research on the link between culture and performance at the

[17] The Engagement Institute. "DNA of Engagement: How Organizations Can Foster Employee Ownership of Engagement." https://www.conference-board.org/dna-engagement2017/

University of South Florida concluded, "Culture causes performance, not vice versa."[18]

Is Your Culture Safety-Based or Fear-Based?

If the following conditions describe your business, chances are good that you have a culture with strong psychological safety. If not, you may have some work to do.

- **Healthy conflict.** Opposing opinions are encouraged and shared. Team members are able to disagree and work it out. Disagreements are about issues, not people, and handled in the spirit of mutual support and excellence.

- **Absence of crises.** Problems are routinely identified and addressed in their earliest stages. People are not constantly putting out fires.

- **Mutual encouragement.** People support and challenge each other to provide better solutions and perform at a higher level.

- **Acknowledgment.** People at every level understand and appreciate each others' contributions, both formally and informally.

- **Performance beyond expectations is the norm.** Team members keep their brains and efforts engaged to get the job done well, not just to check the "done" box.

- **Smooth information flow.** People give and receive

---

[18] Boyce, Anthony S., Levi R. G. Nieminen, Michael A. Gillespie, Ann Marie Ryan, and Daniel R. Denison. "Which Comes First, Organizational Culture or Performance? A Longitudinal Study of Causal Priority with Automobile Dealerships." *Journal of Organizational Behavior*. January 15, 2015.

information freely and appropriately. They neither hoard it nor overwhelm others with it.

- **Happy clients.** How people treat each other within your walls is the best predictor for how they treat people outside your walls. This includes your clients, vendors, and community. As Stephen R. Covey famously said, *"Always treat your employees exactly as you want them to treat your best customers."*[19]

Agree on How

Your organization has a unique blend of personalities, needs, opportunities, and circumstances. Behaviors that create safety in one organization may evoke fear in another. The path to safety is one of dialogue, listening, and mutual agreement.

There is no substitute for working together to develop agreed-upon guidelines for team behaviors that can create the safety for high performance to happen in your organization.

Creating psychological safety is not a one-and-done. As situations, conditions, and team members change, you'll need to continuously evolve this agreement. Most important is to translate the agreement into action. This is not an agreement to put in writing and into a drawer or binder. This is an agreement to be lived daily, discussed frequently, hired for consistently, and challenged as needed.

---

[19] Covey, Stephen R. *The 7 Habits of Highly Effective People: Personal Workbook.* London: Simon & Schuster, 2005.

What You Are Agreeing To

Gather your team and hammer out what you need to have in place for people to feel safe enough to do their best work. Here are nine safety-generating questions to get you started:

1. **How will we be conscious of our impact on others?** In high-performing organizations, people have an awareness that their mindsets, words, and actions can either streamline or impede others—and they strive for the former.

2. **How will we create the conditions for respect and trust?** Respect and trust can't be forced. People can, however, agree to the behaviors that create the environment for respect and trust to thrive. These may include listening and seeking to understand others' needs and viewpoints.

3. **How will we treat errors and mistakes?** Everyone makes mistakes. If you blame, judge, shame, or punish people for errors, you can expect less creativity, less honesty, less problem-solving—and more mistakes. Work out a shared mindset that makes it easy to acknowledge, accept and address blunders, and get back on track. How you treat people when the unwanted happens is critical to the success of the business.

4. **How will we deal with disagreements and conflict?** Every organization is made up of people with differing ideas, sensibilities, vantage points, and conflicting priorities. Expect disagreements and conflicts. See their value. They

are essential for anticipating problems, identifying better ways of operating, and more. The goal is not to avoid them, but to agree on how you will navigate, appreciate, and leverage them.

5. **How will we acknowledge effort and other contributions?** Positive feedback does much more than make people feel good. It builds morale and retention. Most importantly, it lets team members know when they are on the right track and what they should continue to do. What kinds of acknowledgment are effective in your organization? What aren't? Get clear on what you will acknowledge—and how—to drive more of the results you want.

6. **How will we challenge each other to do better?** No team can grow to their next level of excellence if team members don't challenge each other to keep stretching their best efforts even further. When employees allow each other to underperform, the result is mediocrity. There are many possible ways to effectively encourage others to improve. Figuring out what works best for the current team is a continuous process that pays big returns.

7. **How will we communicate?** How completely do you communicate with each other? How early? How inclusively? How consistently? Are you considerate? How does your team ensure you are not overcommunicating and overwhelming people with too much information? Communication, consideration, and safety are closely linked. Keeping people

informed in a timely way about situations that affect them makes a difference.

8. **How will we support each other?** What does support mean in your organization? Do you have each other's backs? Are you interested in each other's lives outside of work? Do you demonstrate kindness and caring? How do you deal with people's personal struggles? Do you give them space? Do you offer help? What can people count on in your culture? And is it the same for all?

9. **How will you respect each other's time?** There are few things more damaging to safety than the pervasive and seemingly innocuous disrespect of each other's time. Think about situations in which your time has been disrespected. Did you feel safe to call it out? What were the real costs?

Many years ago, I was working for a large charitable nonprofit. Every week I attended a meeting with twenty-two other people to brief Richard, their extremely hands-off senior vice president. These meetings were very frustrating. Their only purpose was to update Richard. There was no coordination, no decision-making, and no valid benefit for any of us sitting through everyone else's reports.

And yet we did, week after week after week.

To make matters worse, Richard was consistently late. When he wandered in twenty to thirty minutes tardy, he would waste even more time, taking several minutes to connect and share personal chit chat with a few of his closest associates in the room.

Once the meetings began, they generally took three to four hours. They went on so long, people would be called out of the room to other meetings. When it was an absent person's turn to report, we would all have to wait while someone went to find them.

When the meetings finally dispersed, spin-off complaint sessions took place in the bathrooms, the kitchen, and behind closed doors in private offices, where people blew off steam about the waste of their time—which wasted an additional thirty to sixty minutes of the workday.

Can you spot the invisible agreement this organization had in place? It was something like: *We don't openly question seemingly unnecessary practices. We don't challenge senior leadership, even for the good of the business. We don't start on time here. And we don't respect each other's time.*

None of this was unique to this meeting.

This was no soft agreement. I did the math. I added up everyone's salaries and hourly rates and discovered we were wasting nearly $500,000 every year in this one recurring meeting. That was a lot for a nonprofit that had to raise every penny of that money.

In my world, if you see it, you have to say it. So, in the most nonthreatening way possible, I asked Richard, "This meeting is costing the agency half a million dollars a year, and I'm wondering, does this make sense? Isn't there a more efficient way to brief you?"

Of course, it wasn't that Richard wanted to waste everyone's time. He had just never really considered it. The meeting hadn't started as a gathering of twenty-two people. It had simply grown to that size and scope over time. It wasn't anyone's intention, yet no one had thought to question it, and the meeting had become another costly example of "just the way we do things here."

How often do you not question things that have just come to be in your business?

When Richard realized the cost and impact of the meeting, he became very open to coming up with a new system: a happy ending for the agency and every last one of those twenty-two people.

All the invisible agreements are at their most destructive when they remain unexamined and hidden. What kills them is sunshine and fresh air. You've got to get them out in the open and aligned with your desired outcomes. For more on that, read on.

Create a Visible Agreement about Making it Safe to Succeed

Agree on how the team will:

- Be conscious of our impact on others
- Create the conditions for respect and trust
- Accept that people are human and mistakes happen
- Acknowledge the effort and contributions of others
- Challenge each other to be better
- Communicate effectively
- Support each other
- Encourage healthy disagreement and conflict
- Respect each other's time

Safety does not mean being comfortable. In fact, the act of being accountable means taking more risks. It requires courage to step up and take more ownership for delivering outcomes. That's why we need safety.

—Annie Hyman Pratt

The Third Agreement: What Success Looks Like

▶ THE NEW RULE ◀
FINANCIAL GOALS WON'T KEEP YOU THERE— BEHAVIORAL GOALS WILL

Fifteen years ago, Phil left a job at a Big Four accounting firm to start his own. He brought in several small business clients, and as he became busier and busier, he added staff. He wanted a firm that was very different than the Big Four. He wanted people to feel valued, to have work-life balance, and to love coming to work. That's what he created. His people were happy. Phil took good care of them. They worked nine to five. The pressure was lighter than at any other firm in town.

Except for Phil. Phil was burning out. He was the only one without work-life balance. It took a lot of small clients to keep everyone busy. He was doing all the rainmaking, keeping everyone on track, managing the clients and running the firm. The firm was producing about two million a year, about ten percent of which was profit. That was fine, but only if he wanted to keep up this pace forever—which he most definitely did not. Phil needed some relief.

Phil wanted the other accountants to generate their own books of business, not just for the firm, but for their own careers. He needed them to take more ownership of the workflow. Phil wanted to see them all earn more. To do this, they would need some larger clients. He'd asked his team to develop business. He'd been asking for years. He'd set financial goals for them. But he had made only incremental progress because the new business that came in was still due exclusively to his own effort.

After a health scare, Phil called me and explained his situation.

We gathered the team for an off-site retreat. Together, we brainstormed a picture of success for a new level of performance in the firm. We described what that would look like for the clients, for the individual accountants, for Phil, and for the firm itself. We didn't just talk about financials, but about what people would be doing differently and how they would think differently to create a new way of being that produced new results. We worked out priorities and made action plans. I taught them how to track their progress. We set up ongoing coaching support.

Three months later, every member of the team had made progress on business development. The firm had brought in eight new clients and had become more efficient in moving work through. Profits had more than doubled. By August, they had surpassed the prior year's revenues.

This is the power of a behavioral picture of success.

Why Financial Goals Make for an Incomplete Picture of Success

Early in my first career as a copywriter in the advertising business, I was producing work for a large Internet service provider. The account manager gave my partner and me an assignment; it stated our objective was to increase revenues on a service line by 12 percent.

We had no idea what to do with this input.

So we did what we usually did in response to metric-driven input: We completely ignored it. We then did what we thought made the most sense, which meant that presenting our work to the client was generally hit or miss. As often as not, the client's response was, "This isn't what we were expecting!" (rarely our desired outcome).

The numerical goal had set us up to underperform.

It's understandable that many people in business think financials or other metrics are the desired outcomes. After all, financials and other metrics are what companies are graded on, what stakeholders and shareowners look for, and what pays salaries and bills.

Yet, I don't know anyone who can directly produce a financial or metric result.

This is why we need to make a distinction between financial results and behavioral desired outcomes, or pictures of success.

Financial results are always the byproducts of some set of conditions. It is not possible to go directly to a twelve-percent return. People who are executing on a strategy can only create *the conditions* that will produce that return.

This is why an effective picture of success or desired outcome consists of the desired results (financial and otherwise) combined with the new behaviors and thinking needed to produce those results.

Legend has it that revered former UCLA head basketball coach,

John Wooden, who led his team to ten NCAA championships in twelve years, never coached his players to win a game. He focused only on their passing and their shooting and their free throws and their plays, and especially their teamwork.

Winning leaders put their focus not on results themselves, but instead on the full picture of conditions, thinking, and actions that will create a picture of success.

Becoming Our Picture of Success

Postmodernist writer John Barth, in his masterpiece *Chimera,* wrote, "The key to the treasure *is* the treasure."[20] To me, this means that the key is what we must seek, as opposed to the treasure itself. The key produces treasure over and over, whereas the treasure itself is a one-time deal. The quarterly numbers can't be changed after the fact. But an outcome is a state of being that is ongoing. Numerical results are not sustainable on their own. Behavioral outcomes are.

As leaders, we need to create sustainability by facilitating our teams in finding their key. The first step is creating a clear picture of not only what the treasure looks like, but also what the key looks like—and what we need to do differently and how we need to think differently to obtain the key.

Any discussion of sustainability must include talk of habits. If Phil's team, having doubled their revenues, regressed back to their old behaviors, the financial results would also return to something that resembled the firm's prior state. Sustainability is all about creating new

---

[20] Barth, John. *Chimera*. London: Deutsch, 1974.

habits that team members can own, embody, and repeat.

And we are not just talking about individual habits, but organizational ones—habits of interaction, habits of execution—how people work together to produce results.

An articulated picture of success that includes not only desired results, not only the conditions that will create them, but also new habits of thought, behavior, and interaction gives us the key to unlock treasure after treasure.

This requires a shift from seeing outcomes as external. The external part of outcomes is only a byproduct. What we really want—our key—is a state of being. In order to reach the goal, we have to embody the goal.

Let Reality Inform Your Picture of Success

In every situation, forces beyond your organization's control affect its ability to perform and produce results. Let's call these forces "reality." Reality includes things like the economy, the weather, government regulations, competitive threats, changes in technology, health issues, and so on.

Because we don't have the power to change reality, achieving our picture of success depends on our ability to adapt and work with or around these forces. So if we are committed to delivering on our mission, we need to start with a good understanding of the realities we face. This means looking at what matters that we can't control and figuring out how the organization needs to adapt.

Successful adaptation almost always involves how we think and what we do; behaviors are the core of any effective picture of success. Any approach that doesn't incorporate how the team will respond to outside forces is not going to be an effective solution.

In Phil's situation, health issues beyond his control drove the need for change in the firm. When he presented this context to his staff, they didn't question either that change was necessary or their own involvement in it. They simply mobilized.

In the nonprofit I worked with, described in the last chapter, facing the reality of a half-million-dollar cost for one ongoing meeting—and the burning need for those dollars to be put to work elsewhere—drove Richard and the team to make necessary changes, where years of griping and inconvenience had done nothing.

Being Outcome-Driven Can Inspire a Whole New Way of Thinking and Being

Outcome orientation means understanding the relationship between organizational behavior and results: no more reaction mode and no more arbitrary goals, which are difficult for people to align behind and act upon.

This is about getting clear regarding what is, and responding to it. Recognizing the truth of the situation (which too many businesses miss) is the starting point for achieving any effective picture of success. That the changes required are determined by forces beyond our control makes the need to respond clear, necessary, and nonnegotiable. Clarity aligns people and removes resistance. If you're not responding to the truth of the situation, you are dead in the water.

Begin to recognize the forces operating on your business. Look for those things that affect your ability to produce results. Allow these to reveal the behavior changes your team needs to stay on track toward the realization of your mission.

The Case for a Shared Picture of Success

The FreshBiz business simulation experience is played as a game that looks something like Monopoly, but every aspect of gameplay shines a light on the thinking, actions, and interactions that come into play to support or block success in the business world.

In a recent simulation, one team spent the entire game going in circles in the first quadrant of the game board. The players were so focused on accumulating their own money, avoiding their own costs, acquiring their own property, and trying new strategies to solve their own perceived problems, they completely forgot about the game's objective—to reach the winning space in the fourth quadrant within ninety minutes.

The thinking we use when we have the big picture in mind is vastly different than the thinking we use when we are focused on smaller-picture problems, processes, or tasks. When we lose sight of what we are ultimately going after, it's very easy for challenges—or opportunities—to take us off track, and sometimes far off track.

In the game, teams that request it are coached to first get clear on their desired outcomes—not only on the object of the game but also on how they need to think and act in order to win. This helps them to become aware of options they hadn't considered, evaluate them effectively, identify what they need as well as what they *don't* need, and decide how they will work together to reach their goal. Without exception, teams that do this end up supporting each other in staying on track to win the game—usually with time to spare and a surplus of resources. And they have more fun doing it.

Desired Outcomes Are Agreements

During another recent simulation with a group of graduate students, the group quickly realized that everyone could win and that working together was essential.

In the debrief following the game, Will, one of the players on the only team that did not complete (win) the game, shared that he had played against his teammates and hadn't realized that they could collaborate.

"Interesting," I said. "Did you hear everyone else talking about working together to win?"

"I heard it," he said. "I just didn't agree."

This happens in business every day. When leaders dictate desired outcomes without creating (and verifying) agreement, we end up with people who don't agree and therefore don't align.

Think of times you have not agreed with something you were told to do. You probably felt resistance and frustration. You may have become confused. You possibly moved more slowly. Perhaps you did something different, even opposite, of what you had been told to do.

It likely wasn't your intention to be an obstructionist or disrespectful or not a team player. You simply didn't agree. Maybe with good reason. Maybe with *great* reason.

For an organization to create the conditions that will lead to desired results, the people working in the organization need to individually and collectively embody the thinking and behaviors that create these conditions.

This is why the desired outcome must be an agreement.

Agreement versus Consensus: A Critical Distinction

I can hear some of you thinking, "Wait a minute. It could take literally forever before everyone in my company would be able to agree on the same outcomes."

Let's take a moment to distinguish between consensus and agreement. For our purposes, let's define "consensus" as getting everyone to share the same opinion of what we *should* do. Let's use "agreement" to mean bringing people into alignment about what we each *will* do that is consistent with our reality-based desired outcome. Now, the agreement can happen easily and organically.

Behavioral Desired Outcomes Drive Success Ten Ways (at Least)

Several years ago, I consulted with a manufacturing company in which there were two distinct camps. The younger group was committed to leading-edge statistical modeling: letting the numbers set the direction. The old-timers felt strongly that there was no substitute for the judgment and creativity of the engineers; after all, eyeballing it had worked for them for decades.

When these two groups were pitted against each other, they

were pulling the company in different directions and spending a lot of time and money in conflict and stagnation. While it seemed that their viewpoints were completely oppositional, once a clear shared picture of success was put in place for the organization, there was room for them to peacefully collaborate and for the company to benefit financially and culturally from both schools of thought.

Allowing for a bigger vision is just one of many ways aligning your organization behind clear behavioral outcomes supports success. Here are ten more things behavioral outcomes do for your business:

1. **Create roadmaps**. A behavioral picture of success creates clear direction and alignment, as well as the ability to recognize when you are off-course.

2. **Provide leading indicators**. A financial result is always a lagging indicator. You can never change the past. Behavioral outcomes let you change the future.

3. **Enable sustainability**. Have you ever lost weight only to regain it—plus more? Have you ever had a great quarter followed by a bad one? If we don't permanently change our habits, we tend to return to old ways and old results. Behavioral pictures of success set us up to create new habits, not just new results.

4. **Empower management**. If you've ever tried to change a habit, you know how difficult it is to change your own behavior, let alone someone else's. And no one but the person who holds an attitude can change it. Yet this is what

management is called on to accomplish every day. Agreeing to a clear picture of success goes a long way toward aligning the attitudes and habits of the workforce. When expectations are created *by* the team, there is greater commitment and support for behavior change. It's also cleaner and easier for managers to evaluate and provide feedback on performance.

5. **Focus effort and save time**. When team members know specifically what behaviors and outcomes are expected, it becomes much more clear when time, effort, and resources are being wasted on things that are not aligned. It's also easier and faster to refocus.

6. **Build engagement and alignment**. Clarity engages people. It inspires. It makes team members feel they're part of something bigger than themselves. And that's contagious. Behavioral desired outcomes build a culture of engagement.

7. **Support great hires**. Share your organization's picture of success with prospective employees and you will learn a lot. The clarity of what success looks like will attract (and repel) the right people, set clear expectations right from the start and help you make better hiring decisions. And it's a great differentiator between you and other companies that might be competing for your candidates.

8. **Turbocharge sales**. Give prospective clients a strong, compelling sense of what it would be like to work with your company. Your picture of success will tell clients what you

will literally do for them. It establishes your company as principled, clear, organized leaders. It builds credibility and sets you apart in a positive way.

9. **Improve customer service**. The shift to clearly articulated behavioral desired outcomes is all about creating sustainable financial results through behaviors that work for the clients and the business. It should be no surprise that improved customer service and better retention for both external and internal customers are predictable side effects.

10. **Fuel accountability**. In his books and in his work with global organizations, Mark Samuel of IMPAQ Corporation proposes a new, blameless definition of accountability: *the ability to count on each other to take action that is consistent with agreed-upon desired outcomes.* Think about the elegant simplicity of this for a moment. People are either taking action that is consistent, or they aren't. Describing what we are trying to create in behavioral terms makes accountability easier to understand and deliver.

What a Picture of Success Looks Like (What You're Agreeing To)

Your picture of success will be a word picture that describes all your desired outcomes, not merely the financial ones. It will tell everyone on the team about the *future* that the organization wants to create—not the present, no matter how great the present may be. These desired outcomes are behavioral, identifying what people will be doing differently to create the new future.

Agreement means that everyone will hold this picture of success as a nonnegotiable, and that every team member has ownership and will be accountable for taking the actions that are consistent with the picture you created together. Perhaps most importantly, you are agreeing to keep this picture of success front and center in meetings and conversations, as a North Star, to keep the organization on track.

Your next step is agreeing on priorities to accomplish this picture of success. Read on.

Create a Visible Agreement about What Success Looks Like:

Agree on how the team will:

- Create a clear picture of success
- Base the picture on the desired future state, not only the financials
- Focus on the new thinking and behaviors required
- Hold the picture of success as a nonnegotiable
- Be accountable for taking action that is consistent with the picture
- Use the picture of success to stay on track

*Organizational accountability is the ability
to count on each other to take actions
that are consistent with agreed-upon desired
outcomes.*

—**Mark Samuel**

The Fourth Agreement: Where We Will Put Our Shared Attention

▶ THE NEW RULE ◀
A FEW NONNEGOTIABLE PRIORITIES WILL ACCOMPLISH MORE THAN YOU THINK POSSIBLE

You know what it's like when people aren't on the same page? Salma was dealing with this in spades. She had been hired by Gerry, the CEO of a large Midwestern health care system, to fix a broken merger with a specialty hospital it had acquired more than two years earlier. She had landed the position of president of the hospital because she was globally respected as a physician. But she had never taken a company through a cultural integration before. She knew the importance of getting people aligned for a merger to succeed; she also knew that her experience wouldn't be sufficient. So Salma brought my company in to assist.

When I asked my typical first question—"What would success look like?"—Salma didn't have a ready answer. You see, she had been getting mixed messages from Gerry and the other leaders in the hospital system.

Like many health system CEOs, Gerry was under a lot of pressure due to changes in the industry and was navigating a world of competing priorities. Increasing competition meant the organization needed to establish a strong brand presence beyond its market by keeping services at a world-class level. Changes in the law were leading Gerry to see a shift from fee-for-service to value-based care, which meant change at every level of the organization. As a result, Gerry was driving many simultaneous reconfigurations: consolidating services, shifting inpatient programs to outpatient, streamlining electronic records systems that weren't connected enterprise-wide, and much more.

Each of these initiatives required capital. Due to global economic challenges, there had been significant reductions in reimbursements, grants, and philanthropic support, which meant the system had far fewer resources to accomplish these objectives. So even as Gerry was leaning on the hospital presidents to build revenues, he was pressing the system CFO to reduce expenses, which in turn caused her to cut budgets and demand dramatic expense reductions from these very same hospital presidents.

All this put Salma in a tough spot. She needed to integrate the hospital with the system and to simultaneously increase its revenues and reduce its expenses. This meant, in part, renegotiating physician contracts and holding physicians accountable for running profitable practices.

The doctors would need to handle more patients, work longer hours, take on more responsibility, and—adding insult to injury—endure significant pay cuts. Salma needed to get them to do all this without losing them to her competition, because, after all, without physicians, there is no hospital.

Of course, physicians were pushing back. They wanted higher, not lower, compensation for their increased efforts. They demanded more, not fewer, resources. They were more and more frustrated by the amount of time it was taking to keep electronic records up to date and to comply with new privacy and security standards. They were concerned that packing in so many patients, and spending less time with each one, made them and the hospital vulnerable to missing something important.

Patient unhappiness with all these circumstances was showing up where it hurt most: in patient satisfaction scores that directly impacted the hospital's Medicare reimbursement rates, their reputation, and their bottom line. Getting those scores up was yet another initiative Gerry added to Salma's long list of goals.

Can you spot the invisible agreements?

They were trying to do everything at once. Each group in the system had completely different and often competing priorities. Everyone was working in their own separate silos trying to serve their own disconnected needs.

They didn't discuss their objectives and conflicting priorities as a team. Instead, they tried to manage and manipulate each other—and push off any consequences as long as possible.

This is how things had always been done. And that was why, two years into the merger, from the top to the bottom of the food chain, no one was getting their needs, wants, or priorities met.

No organization can perform effectively, let alone at its highest level, when team members are pulling in opposite directions and fighting each other for control. The results will always be conflict, a tug-of-war over resources and focus, and failure to move forward with the clarity and propulsion that alignment provides.

Shared Priorities Make the Difference

The year was 2010. The Affordable Care Act (a.k.a. "Obamacare") had just been signed. The health benefits industry was in upheaval with total uncertainty and fear of unpredictable price increases.

Thelma was the owner of a health benefits advisory firm with a big hairy audacious vision. She wanted to change people's insurance experience. She saw no reason the health insurance process couldn't be simple, easy, and even have certainty under these conditions. She had a million ideas about how to achieve this. In fact, she had a list of twenty-three ongoing projects, many of which had been on her team's to-do list for the past three years.

What with the ongoing daily demands of current work and fielding clients' panicked phone calls, her team could only make a little headway on a project at a time. Each project had moved forward incrementally, but none were even close to being up and running. Everyone was working exceptionally long hours, and there had been turnover of some key people, making it even harder to keep all the projects alive. Thelma felt burned out.

She realized something had to change. And she knew she needed support. Thelma and I had worked together in the past. She called me and we gathered her team. Together, we described their picture of success and listed all the improvements needed to achieve it. We evaluated where they stood on each one.

We identified the three most powerful initiatives that would have the greatest impact on both clients and the firm. These would be nonnegotiables. They would take precedence over everything else in the company's attention, decision-making, and follow-up. We also assigned five secondary projects that were important, but would only get attention when the top priorities were moving forward according to plan. We established a meeting process for identifying and solving problems to keep the priorities on track. Thelma and I continued to meet periodically for coaching.

Three months later, the team had accomplished not only the top three priorities *and* the five secondary priorities, but also a full fourteen of the projects on her list for the whole year.

Less is literally more. Focus makes all the difference.

Watch Out for These Invisible Agreements

It's easy to get trapped in a hidden game that keeps your organization from focusing on what's most important. Invisible agreements can actually block you from accomplishing your most important initiatives. Here are just a few patterns to look out for:

- **Not establishing priorities at all:** Eric is the owner of an architecture firm. The firm had been through a tough year, and it was obvious to Eric that everyone's focus needed to be on developing new business. He assumed everyone knew this. However, everyone else was hoping that Eric was working on that while instead Eric was focused on the day-to-day demands of running the business. As a result, no one was creating new opportunities.

- **Too many conflicting priorities:** June is an administrator in Salma's health care organization. She is personally responsible for developing and getting the annual budget approved, renegotiating physician contracts, reorganizing departments, dealing with staff threats to unionize, preparing for Joint Commission accreditation, and responding to rising physician issues and complaints. June typically works an eighty-hour week. When crises happen in more than one area (almost every day), she has to choose arbitrarily what gets her attention and what gets ignored. Everything is a priority. And there are constantly priority areas in crisis. When everything is a priority, nothing is a priority.

- **Constantly changing priorities:** Greg is the executive director of a tech strategy firm. At the beginning of each month, he meets with the owner, Sylvia, to review priority projects. Like clockwork, within a few days of that meeting, he will get an email from Sylvia with an idea that "occurred to her that morning" that she wants him to "drop everything to pursue." This pattern repeats with new directions every few days. By the time the next monthly meeting rolls around, a completely new set of priorities has supplanted those they agreed upon the previous month. This happens month after month. Little has actually been accomplished. Greg is frustrated and resentful, and Sylvia's confidence in Greg is waning. They aren't alone. Many organizations experience this kind of costly mission creep.

- **Problem-driven or fear-driven priorities:** Doris inherited leadership of a skilled nursing facility that has been in her family for three generations. Like most other businesses in this field, there are many threats to their viability. They are operating on very thin margins, reimbursements are declining, and the facility is losing patients to the competition because it desperately needs an update. On top of that, evolving technology is making it possible for more and more people to recover at home and the number of potential patients decreases each year. Doris lives in a constant state of fear that she will preside over the end of her family's legacy. This drives her to make cutting expenses her primary focus, rather than spending money on the facility, the right staff, or training. This fear-driven focus is magnifying the problem and blinding her to potentially effective solutions.

- **Priorities that don't connect with desired outcomes:** Ten years ago, Ben founded a small nonprofit that provides warm, personal services for disabled youth in a small region of a large metropolitan area. In recent years, he'd become so strapped for cash and other resources that he found himself forced to partner with a larger, more institutional nonprofit. He told his leadership team that his top priority was to maintain their unique culture, no matter what. Unfortunately, this direction clearly set up conflict with their new partner and might even obstruct the purpose of the partnership—to provide more services for their constituents. If a priority is not aligned with the desired outcomes, it has no business being a priority.

- **Uncommunicated priorities:** The leadership team at a financial investment company meets annually to determine their priorities for the year. They take copious notes and then go back to doing exactly what they were doing the year before. The rest of the company is blissfully unaware that anything has changed. And nothing does. What you don't communicate (over and over) doesn't move forward.

- **Shadow priorities:** In his reporting to investors, the CEO of a hot tech startup states the top priority is getting their product to market. In practice, what is most important to him is becoming famous. He hires people according to the amount of press they have generated in the past, rather than their knowledge or ability to get the job done. He is frequently unavailable to make critical decisions because he is spending his time juggling photo shoots and press interviews. His lack of availability causes confusion in the organization and long delays in meeting their stated objective. It doesn't matter what you *say* your priorities are—priorities are actually determined by what you *do*.

Three Signs That Your Priorities Need Work

1. **Recurring priorities:** When the same priorities show up year after year after year.

2. **Burnout:** Excessive sick days; staff turnover; increases in errors, accidents, and conflicts; reduced efficiency; low motivation and/or morale.

3. **Cycles of abandonment and control:** A pattern of ignoring something until a crisis arises, at which point people mobilize to address the problem and get things back under control. Everyone breathes a sigh of relief and shifts their full attention to the next crisis.

A 2011 Booz & Company study[21] showed that as an executive team's priority list grows, their revenue growth declines. The reverse is also true: executives with the most focused strategic priorities (one to three) were most likely to report above-average revenue growth.

What You Are Agreeing To

Developing shared priorities means that you will collectively elevate a select few goals, initiatives, and/or projects as more important than the rest for an agreed upon time period. When other demands

---

[21] Leinwand, Paul and Cesare Mainardi. "Stop Chasing Too Many Priorities." *Harvard Business Review*, April 14, 2011. https://hbr.org/2011/04/stop-chasing-too-many-prioriti.

conflict with these priorities, you will address the priority items first and deal with the consequences without blame or judgment. You are committing to accomplish these most important initiatives no matter what it takes.

How you accomplish those priorities *is* negotiable. What isn't negotiable is committing to planning, action, problem-solving and follow-through until they are complete. Everyone in the organization has ownership of and accountability for doing this—which means you are in this together and you will support each other in removing obstacles and taking actions that lead to success.

Don't Forget Improvement Priorities

The temptation in most businesses is to focus on business priorities—those work projects that generate revenues. These are certainly important. But it's also crucial to remember that the world continues to move forward and grow around us. Competitors spring up. New customer needs arise. New knowledge comes into being.

Even as you are working on this year's numbers and goals, you also must focus on the future by including improvement projects in your priorities; it's critical for long-term success.

What If Priorities Need to Change?

Sometimes things beyond your control will dictate a change in what's important. While you don't want to take changing priorities lightly, you also don't want the organization dogmatically chasing objectives that are no longer relevant.

One of the most important things to agree upon right from the start (or as soon as possible) is *how* you will go about changing priorities when needed. As a team, determine:

- What conditions justify a change?
- Who needs to be involved?
- How will the change in priorities be communicated?

When you have a plan in place, and everybody is aware of it, these kinds of changes can be incorporated seamlessly and painlessly.

Owning Priorities Is Not for the Faint of Heart

Clare owns a specialized technology consulting firm. They are a one-client firm, which makes them vulnerable. The team established a priority project of landing new clients so if anything went wrong with their anchor client, they wouldn't be out of business. They brought in a series of business development people who supposedly had contacts in their target audience. For many reasons none of these people worked out. After several failed attempts, their frustration and fear of yet another failure led to complete stall-out. A year later, they lost the big client and had to scramble to significantly downsize and completely restructure in order to stay alive.

As we move toward our growth goals, uncomfortable situations are often a part of the process. When we encounter discomfort, it's human nature to seek comfort and safety. And in seeking comfort, we often abandon priorities without even realizing we have done so.

The best way to prevent this from happening is by agreement. When we have agreed as a group upon what is most important, nonnegotiable, and how we are going to follow up, shared accountability keeps us on track, even when our comfort zones threaten to pull us off.

In the messy real world of business, you will be confronted by all kinds of vicious challenges to your priorities. Staying the course takes inner strength, commitment, and support in the face of breakdowns, especially when short-term needs present immediate threats or opportunities.

Business is a team sport. It takes a team to fight off all the attacks on the organization's priorities. This is why agreements are critical and shared desired outcomes are essential. Develop and agree upon your priorities, and results will far exceed the mere accomplishment of those goals.

Setting and agreeing on priorities builds cultural character. It matures and professionalizes your organization, provides direction, and develops focus, alignment, and clarity. It creates stronger teams and improves morale, engagement, and commitment. It provides the discipline of measurement and accountability.

Next step: the roles people will play and the crucial interconnections between team members, departments, and divisions in executing on your priorities.

Create a Visible Agreement About Where You'll Put Your Shared Attention

Agree on how the team will:

- Select the top priorities for organizational focus
- Make the accomplishment of these priorities nonnegotiable
- Ensure that when these conflict with other demands, team members will address priorities first and accept the consequences without blame or judgment
- Share ownership of and accountability for priorities
- Commit to accomplishing these, no matter what it takes
- Commit to continued planning, action, problem solving, follow-up, and follow-through until complete
- Support each other by removing obstacles
- Include teamwork and execution improvement in organizational priorities
- Know when it is appropriate to change a priority

Simple can be harder than complex: You have to work hard to get your thinking clean to make it simple. But it's worth it in the end because once you get there, you can move mountains.

—Steve Jobs

The Fifth Agreement:
Who Does What—And How

YOU CAN'T DEFINE ROLES WITHOUT DEFINING HOW PEOPLE AND TEAMS WORK TOGETHER

Throughout high school, my son played football on a Southern California high school team. One of the players on an opposing team was a gifted superstar; he was big and strong, a formidable opponent. But his ego kept him from being a team player. After one big loss, a local reporter interviewing the players asked him, "What went wrong?"

"I don't know!" he responded defiantly. "I did *my* job!"

His job was to block the player in front of him. He had done that and then stood back and watched angrily as his teammates failed. What he missed was that his role was to be part of a unit that protected the quarterback. By focusing solely on his *job*, this player had become disconnected from his *role* and the team's desired outcome.

This same phenomenon occurs daily in businesses around the world. Team members perceive their roles as individual executions of their jobs, literally separated from the rest of the organization.

It may seem obvious that jobs exist to serve the big picture of the organization. But this is one of many obvious truths which organizations simply don't put into practice. How often are staff members, and even entire teams or departments, disconnected from the big picture? The cost of this disconnect is painfully expressed in disengagement, wasted effort, missed objectives, and much more.

Role Clarity: It's Not What You Think

In the hospital run by Salma, discussed in the previous chapter, the senior leadership team was made up of the president, chief administrative officer, chief operating officer, chief medical officer, and controller. Each would have told you he or she was absolutely clear on the role he or she played in the organization and as part of the leadership team. After all, each had many years of experience in both current and past positions.

However, they daily found themselves butting heads and working at conflicting purposes. Relationships within the team had eroded, trust was low, and communication was treated as a necessary evil to be avoided whenever possible. This had a profound impact on the hospital's ability to serve its patients, to meet its financial objectives, and to function effectively.

When you see breakdowns like these happening between people, that's a sure sign that if role clarity exists at all, it is compromised.

Most people misunderstand role clarity and think roles are clear even when they are not. In fact, in the business world, most of us have learned to equate job titles, descriptions and duties with roles. But these are not the same thing. When we think they are the same, we tend to ignore roles—with painful and often disastrous results.

Let's first get the language straight.

A job title is a very brief, often hierarchical description of a person's position in an organization. The same titles can mean very different things in different organizations or even different departments. People often mistake job titles for roles, thinking that CEO, marketing manager, or VP of sales are roles.

Job descriptions are broad, general, written statements defining a specific job. They generally include tasks, duties, responsibilities, and scope, as well as the name or designation of the person to whom the employee reports. The key words here are *broad* and *general*. In other words, a job description can apply to anyone in the same position.

Job duties are the tasks a person must accomplish as part of his or her job. Job responsibilities are the functions an employee performs. Competencies are the strengths and areas of expertise required to be successful in a job. Key behaviors are the actions which, if carried out appropriately, are assumed to lead to appropriate results.

Roles, on the other hand, include and transcend all these to describe the part people play within the organization—the purpose they serve in the big picture of the business. Roles incorporate the interconnections and interdependencies people need to maintain and navigate to their part in the process of helping the organization realize its purpose.

A simple example: *Receptionist* is a job title. The job description might be "To manage incoming phone calls and greet visitors." The duties of a receptionist might include answering phones, taking messages, providing callers with information, and directing visitors to the appropriate personnel. A receptionist's competencies might include communication skills, customer service, and technical aptitude with phone systems. Some key behaviors might be smiling, taking criticism with grace, and gathering pertinent information from callers. However, the *role* of the receptionist is to be the gatekeeper, protecting people in the organization from unnecessary distractions and ensuring they are prepared to respond effectively to callers and visitors.

Can you see the distinction—and the importance of the distinction—as well as the importance of clarity in knowing what role each person is there to play?

In a sense, roles are like gravity. Gravity exists, whether or not we are aware of it. If we are conscious of gravity, then we can learn to work with and around it, as astronauts, pilots, and athletes do daily. If we are unaware of it, gravity works against us and keep us down. When team members are conscious of the interconnections and interdependencies between themselves and others, they have powerful information that can help them adapt their actions and interactions to help everyone perform at a higher level. Lack of awareness of roles can only act to hold the organization down.

A survey of 25,000 managers and supervisors found that the top three reasons people do not do what they are supposed to on the job is that "1. They don't know why they should do it; 2. They don't know how to do it; 3. They don't know what they are supposed to do."[22] When we

---

[22] Fournies, Ferdinand F. *Why Employees Don't Do What They're Supposed to Do...and What to Do About It.* New York: McGraw-Hill, 2007.

don't define the expected behaviors associated with a role and leave them to chance, what results is often not a fit.

Ever notice that businesses tend to hire people for their skills and fire them for their behavior? Two out of every five new CEOs fail in their first eighteen months on the job. This is because they fail to establish a cultural fit; they fail to build teamwork with staff and peers and they are unclear about what what their board expects.[23] All these reasons are related to roles (and interactions) and not covered in job descriptions.

Roles Are About Interconnections

The workplace is a network of interconnections and interdependencies. Because whatever a business focuses on will likely grow, organizations need to build in the ability to leverage an increasing number of peoples' knowledge, skills, and efforts. This is why team members need to understand not only their own roles, but also those of others, for the business to achieve and sustain high performance.

Most organizations approach roles individual by individual. But the purpose of working as an organization is to leverage the skills, knowledge, and efforts of a *multitude* to produce a result *together*. Even individual contributors don't really work alone.

There is a distinction to be made between interactions (which are transactional) and relationships (which are emotional). How people transact (collaborate, consult, share information) and how they relate (demonstrate knowing, caring, and respect) affects the roles they play. Without shared clarity about both interactions and relationships,

---

[23] Masters, Brooke. "Rise of a Headhunter," *Financial Times.* March 30, 2009. https://www.ft.com/content/19975256-1af2-11de-8aa3-0000779fd2ac

breakdowns happen. Team members will duplicate efforts and overstep boundaries. They will fail to leverage everyone's abilities and prevent optimal performance.

When team members understand and care how their behaviors impact others and the organization's objectives, the organization has established a critical piece of the foundation for maximum performance.

Roles Exist to Serve Desired Outcomes

Organizations exist to produce outcomes. Everything organizations do must be in service to those outcomes, either directly or indirectly. Yet it's easy to get caught in the trap of filling positions just because they are on an org chart, whether or not they are still needed. It's common for organizations to create positions and convoluted reporting structures out of convenience even as they lose track of the goals of the business. All too often, businesses wind up with bloated organizations and complex reporting structures that actually get in the way of getting the work done.

Roles Are Inseparably Intertwined with Invisible Agreements

In the weekly staff meetings of a manufacturing company, Charlie is always the guy who raises the problem everyone sees but doesn't have the guts to say. When conversations turn negative, Suzanne acts as the peacemaker, moving everyone back into mutual respect. When they get off track, Rosario calls it out and reminds the group what they are there to accomplish. Perhaps most interestingly, when

Suzanne is on vacation, and a conflict breaks out, Jenna steps in to play peacemaker.

This group dynamic might sound like it is based on personality—and that is certainly part of what informs the roles we play. Charlie, Suzanne, Rosario, and Jenna each slipped into these roles without intention. Now they own them. It's become an invisible agreement among them.

Because so many of the agreements about how we work together are unspoken—and as a rule, we are unaware of their existence—we step into roles unconsciously, usually with little thought or discussion. And we define our roles in part by the roles others play. This has implications that go far beyond keeping a meeting on track.

Take this cautionary tale of two partners, who owned a small manufacturing company. James thought his role was to be the "adult in the room," maintaining stability. To him, this meant being extremely frugal, scrutinizing every expense, declining requests that he didn't see as directly connected to revenues, making unilateral decisions, and expecting total compliance.

Larry, his junior by twenty-two years, saw his own role as overcoming the obstacles James put in the path of the growth of the business. For him, this meant sneaking things by James's scrutiny. Sometimes he succeeded. Sometimes he didn't. Frequently, they became locked in protracted battles that could become quite vicious, and dragged others into the maelstrom. People in the company frequently found themselves polarized between the two partners. Staff turnover was high. So was client turnover. The company was neither stable nor growing. Although Larry suggested getting outside help to solve the problem, James was not willing to look at any change in his role or behaviors. Ultimately, the company closed its doors, the victim of poorly defined roles.

Roles Evolve Continuously

People tend to assume that whatever job description was in place at the moment of hiring is what will be in place for their tenure in that position. Nothing could be further from the truth or a better set up for underperformance.

Roles are contextual and need to change as conditions evolve, which means they morph much more quickly than job descriptions, positions, titles, or salaries.

Theresa is the chief nursing officer in a long-term care facility in the southwest. Changes are coming so quickly that she needs to adapt her thinking, actions, and interactions almost every week. Her title and compensation, however, haven't changed in three years.

In a sense, perfect role clarity is impossible. Each of us needs to understand and play many different roles in many different situations. When we aren't aware that roles change with circumstances, we are more likely to force thinking and actions that may have been right for *one* desired outcome onto *all* desired outcomes. Part of the role clarity we need to seek is how to be adaptable in our roles. To not acknowledge or plan for this is to set the organization up for failures.

Mindset Is an Essential Part of Role Definition

In year one of a startup consumer technology company, the senior leadership team's primary role was to propel the company's growth by making key hires and formalizing deals with strategic partners. This endeavor required them to think like the people and partners they wanted to recruit, connect to people and what they valued, and create a compelling experience of their workspace and their vision.

Three years later, after the third round of outside investment, they had the right people in place. The leadership team's primary roles had shifted several times over and the company now needed to focus on getting product ready for market. This required a completely different mindset—much more critical, task-driven, and product- and quality-oriented.

As circumstances change, new purposes, mindsets, behaviors, and interactions (roles) need to be articulated and put into practice, or else they can easily be missed.

Priorities and Roles Go Hand in Hand

After fifteen years in big agencies, Horace started his own boutique advertising and marketing firm. Tiffany was one of his early hires. As in many small businesses, people wore multiple hats. The position he had advertised talked about administrative, sales, and copywriting responsibilities. Tiffany aspired to be a copywriter and saw that as the most important of her three roles. Horace needed all three roles accomplished but felt the sales function was most critical to the success of the firm. Because this wasn't expressly agreed to between them, as Tiffany spent more and more time developing her creative skills, there were frequent misunderstandings, mutual frustration, and struggle—along with failure to meet their sales goals. Once I supported them in working out an agreement about priorities and their impact on Tiffany's roles, both results and relationships improved.

For Best Results, Build in Evaluation

We've all played the game "Hot and Cold." Hot means you're close to finding the hidden object; cold means you aren't. Until a player starts to move, you can't give them any feedback.

When you first work out roles as a team, you won't yet know if you've gotten it right. People will have to start putting their roles into practice before you can tell whether they are getting hotter or colder. And as circumstances and team makeup change, hidden targets will move requiring new direction and role shifts.

Just as organizations need leading indicators to evaluate the effectiveness of a process or strategy, they also need leading indicators for role effectiveness. This is a great reason to build feedback into role clarity.

Five Essential Aspects of Role

1. Interconnected and interdependent
2. Driven by desired outcomes
3. Fundamentally behavioral
4. Evolving continuously
5. Drivers of priorities as well as how we prioritize

Without Role Clarity, There Is No Accountability

We can't be accountable for our own roles or hold others accountable for their roles if the actions and interactions required for those roles haven't been defined. Clear role agreements help people to come to accountability. And when people are not accountable, clear agreements make conversations that correct the situation much easier.

There are many other benefits of having shared and agreed-upon role clarity. Here are just a few:

- Improved collaboration
- Effective decision-making
- Better follow-through
- Smoother workflow
- Increased speed and urgency
- Seamless problem identification and solving
- Accelerated conflict resolution
- Higher morale
- Improved sustainability

Roles Cannot Be Determined Individually

We must give up treating static, isolated job descriptions as the guidelines for the roles people play in business. We need to recognize that roles are dynamic, constantly evolving, and fundamentally interconnected. Our roles affect each other's abilities to function as well as the results we produce. We cannot correctly assume an understanding of role needs, boundaries, and interconnections for others—and we can't work out our own needs, boundaries, and interconnections on our own. As such, the only way a business can successfully get people to play their roles effectively is by working it out together. This means coming to an agreement.

What It Looks Like

After college and a series of frustrating jobs in the tech world, Brad decided to start his own electronics repair business out of his garage. He quickly realized he couldn't do it alone, so he asked his best high school buddies, Charlie and Shawn, to build the business with him. They got off to a good start, landing a big client that enabled them to get a real workspace and hire staff.

That's when the trouble started. It wasn't clear who was going to do what. The partners had different ideas about the ways things should be done, and they would each give staff and vendors mixed messages. This created mass confusion, arguments, and missed deadlines. Sometimes all three would communicate different things to the client and be shocked when the client repeated back what one of the other partners had promised. Conflicts between the three friends started to become a daily occurrence. Team members and suppliers got caught in the crossfire, and for too long they were tolerating the disruptions, having to replace people and vendors. When the big client finally said that if they didn't solve their problems, he was going to have to find another resource, Brad called me.

We blocked out a Saturday and sat down with some easel pads and markers. The partners were all quickly on the same page regarding the picture of success for the business in the coming year. That done, we started to talk about what needed to change, what was most important, and the obstacles they needed to overcome. It took a little doing to get everyone to let go of defensiveness, but they were able to get there. We blocked out the flow of the work, and the communication between them and the rest of the organization. We made judgment and blame against the law and took a look at where the breakdowns were happening. From there, it was relatively obvious where the gaps and overlaps were. With this context, we clarified the roles each partner would play and what each needed to do differently. Brad would be the lead on communicating with the client, Shawn would be the point person for staff communication, and Charlie would take lead on vendor relationships. We worked out the expectations each of the partners would have of each other, as well as how they would deal with matters quickly and supportively when expectations were not met. We wrapped up by identifying some leading indicators for whether the new agreements were working—or not.

The change was immediate. Staff could feel it the minute work began on Monday morning. The role clarity between the partners created stability for the entire organization. The company retained the client. Turnover stopped. Conflicts almost entirely disappeared, and on rare occasions when they did surface, the partners knew what to do and got back on track without much delay. What they didn't expect was the referral their big client made to another big client about six months later, which nearly doubled their revenues. The client shared with Brad that he never would have made that introduction before seeing their operational transformation.

What's next? How your organization will make and follow through on decisions.

Create a Visible Agreement about Who Does What—and How

Agree on how the team will:

- Connect roles with desired outcomes

- Identify and define important interdependencies and mutual expectations

- Identify gaps, areas of overlap, and predictable areas of breakdown

- Work out the required thinking and do-differentlies

- Deal with changing roles as conditions change

- Respond when things don't go as expected

- Know whether defined roles are working

I say you play a part, you don't work one.

—John Hurt

The Sixth Agreement:
How Our Team Will Decide and Follow Through

Tim is the founder and owner of a thirty-year-old logistics company. Clients come to him to plan the flow of their products from point-of-origin to point-of-consumption. He is a brilliant and creative strategic thinker with an active, solution-oriented mind.

When a client called with a potential project, Tim asked the client to walk him through their process. He knew whether a project was a good fit by the flood of ideas triggered during this initial meeting.

When he accepted a project, Tim would race back to the office and gather the team to download information and ideas. Tim has a compelling presence, and his excitement is contagious. The direction he offered always seemed clear and actionable. Decisions were made quickly, and the team would jump into the project with enthusiasm, converting ideas into action and execution plans.

The problem was that Tim would then leave the meetings, having cleared his mind of those first seedlings of ideas, and continue to work on the problems. He would then often develop a whole new set of ideas, along with a mental list of colleagues whose expertise might add value. Then, he would make a series of phone calls and come up with a brand new set of solutions.

At the next staff meeting, as the team reported on their progress, he would be shocked and angry that the team had spent time and money on a strategy that he no longer felt was the right one. And the team would respond with stunned silence—they had merely been following what they thought were his marching orders.

Turnover in this environment was inevitable. It didn't take new employees long to realize the way things worked at the company. Everyone but Tim started each project knowing that a complete turnaround midstream was guaranteed, but also fearful not to take his direction and move forward. Over time, employees became more and more passive in the initial brainstorming process and slower and slower to implement.

Tim, meanwhile, exited each meeting validated in his belief that he had to do all the work himself and needed to go outside the business to get solid input. He thought his employees were not competent, didn't care, and that it all rested on him. He could feel their resentment but didn't see it as justified.

The impact of this dynamic on the business was significant. It failed to retain more than fifty percent of its clients. When interviewed, all these clients reported dissatisfaction; the company's costs always significantly exceeded estimates. Tim was frustrated that margins were lower than they should be, but he didn't see the connection to his own behavior. The team saw that connection clearly but was too fearful to confront him. They felt they had to accept that Tim was Tim, and this was how Tim operated.

This had become their invisible agreement. They did this dance over and over again.

An operations consultant working with Tim on process improvement brought me in to work with the team on these behaviors, which were having a profound impact on their results. I helped the team look at the dynamic without blame or judgment. Together, we negotiated some new agreements about how they made and communicated decisions. We separated the initial brainstorming process from the decision-making process and agreed that nothing would move forward until a subsequent official decision had been made. We established a time frame during which Tim and everyone else could gather additional input and a clear procedure so everyone was on the same page about what was—and wasn't—moving forward.

This was a game changer. Over the next twelve months, the company increased its profit margins. People started to enjoy their work again. Client satisfaction and retention increased dramatically. The company was able to recruit and retain talent. For the first time, everybody was functioning as a real team.

Decisions: The Core Building Blocks of Growth and Change

American entrepreneur, author, and speaker, Jim Rohn once

said, "You cannot make progress without making decisions." Can you think of any aspect of business that doesn't depend on solid decisions for forward movement?

Yet good decision-making depends on much more than just good decisions. Julie is proof. She is one of four consultants who came together to form a firm.

At one point, a networking buddy offered Julie a great deal on some consulting services. Julie saw the opportunity as a no-brainer. There was some investment of time and money required, but she believed the consulting would set them up to succeed as a firm and that all her partners would benefit. She signed the engagement contract.

Can you spot the invisible agreement?

Julie made the decision without consulting her partners, assuming they would agree. Although the decision may ultimately have been a good one, the unilateral process damaged trust between Julie and her partners. In reaction, her partners refused to support the decision. Within a year, Julie and her partners split, and Julie had to rebuild her business from the ground up.

The impact of *how* a business makes its decisions extends far beyond the decisions themselves—much further than most decision-makers know. Every decision has many seen and unseen consequences. Not all are as visible as they were in Julie's situation. But the invisible repercussions can be even more damaging than the visible ones.

Teams and organizations tend to have consistent decision-making patterns. Up until this event, Julie's firm had a pattern of partners making decisions without consulting each other. This led Julie to believe it would be OK for her to do this as well. Yet, Julie's decision crossed a line and ultimately destroyed the partnership. Although it read to the partners as Julie's failure, it was actually the failure of *all* the partners to come to agreement about how they would make decisions that caused the end of their collaboration.

How organizations decide can have positive or negative effects on bottom line results, expenses, margins, workflow, customer service, morale, commitment, employee engagement, and client retention. It's a long list that includes literally every aspect of the business. Anything can be propelled forward or held back based on *how* decisions are handled. Both internal and external perceptions—the brand reputation—of both senior leadership and of the business are often based significantly on how decision-making happens.

The point is that decision-making practices matter.

Recognize Any of these Five Common Decision-Making Patterns?

- **Assumptive decision-making: Assuming a decision has been made when it hasn't.** This is how Tim and his team operated. The cost: reduced profits, wasted time and resources, and expensive turnover.

- **Impulsive decision-making: Not enough information or thought.** Sonja is a charismatic key business leader in a financial services company. A vendor she'd relied on for many years had a new employee mess up a project, making

Sonja look bad to her client. Sonja had recently met another vendor at an industry event. Upon learning of the screw-up, she picked up the phone and hired the new vendor on the spot. Three months later, the very same client called, furious that key components of the new product were weaker and more expensive. They moved their business to Sonja's competitor. This is a perfect example of making an impulsive decision. This wasn't the first time Sonja had found herself in this position. It's not uncommon for strong leaders who want immediate results to have a pattern of jumping too quickly, and making decisions emotionally, without due diligence and considering future ramifications. The cost: bad decisions and breakdowns.

- **Perfectionistic decision-making: Overthinking and Over-researching.** Arthur is a detail-oriented CFO in a manufacturing company. He hates to make mistakes. He feels a responsibility to the CEO and the organization to get it right the first time. He works long hours and scrutinizes spreadsheets. He has a gift for catching errors that has saved the company from risk that represents hundreds of thousands of dollars through the years. The problem is that his team needs to make decisions that affect other departments' effectiveness. While Arthur has agonized over tiny amounts before approving expenditures, the sales team has lost prospective clients, the purchasing department has lost savings opportunities, and various managers have lost prospective talent to the competition—all at costs that have far exceeded the savings Arthur was struggling to realize. There are no perfect decisions. Yet many organizations have an invisible agreement that there are severe consequences for getting things wrong. This means decision-makers must know things *absolutely* before anything can move forward. Of course, it is never possible to predict absolutely how things will go. The cost: project slowdowns and missed opportunities that impact the bottom line.

- **Isolationist decision-making: Failing to involve key people.** Fran is the caring and well-liked director of human resources in an advertising agency that's part of a huge conglomerate. Other members of the leadership team are extremely Type A, driving for results. The agency moves at a breakneck pace and people work extremely long hours. Turnover is considerable, and employee surveys show that people feel unhappy and unappreciated. The CEO, who prides himself on happy employees and recently had read an article about the importance of acknowledgment, instructed Fran to implement a process in which people nominated their colleagues for awards. Fran didn't like this idea. She knew it would single out individuals in power positions and demotivate the support people—the ones who were most unhappy and unappreciated. But no one asked her. It's not the first time that six or twelve months into a failed project, all she can say is, "I could have told you that wouldn't work." Too often, leaders fail to get input from and agreement with the people who are most affected by decisions and accountable for their implementation. Generally, these are the people with the knowledge that can inform a quality decision. The cost: bad decisions and failure to implement decisions.

- **Abandonment decision-making: Decisions without ownership or follow-up plan.** In the current economic climate, a southwestern regional medical center had to confront a growing deficit. The management team decided that, although they had never done so before, it was time to hold their staff physicians accountable for profitability. They knew this would add a significant burden to doctors who were already struggling with the demands of their new electronic medical records system. Everyone agreed it was the right course to take, although no one wanted to have those conversations with the physicians. Together, the leadership team drafted an email to be sent to the entire medical staff. Month after month, however, as they looked at the physicians' numbers, there was no improvement in profitability. Why not? No one had taken ownership of the change. Although they had determined what needed to be done, there was no plan regarding how physician accountability for profitability would be implemented, and there was no follow-through besides reporting on and lamenting the numbers each month. The cost: no change—and the far-reaching costs that come with no forward movement.

And there are even more:

- **Silent decision making:** failing to communicate a decision
- **Ego-driven decision making:** when decisions are driven by the need for power and control rather than by clarity and accountability
- **Agenda-driven decision making:** when decisions are based on personal agendas that have little to do with desired outcomes

What patterns have you observed in your organization?

The Challenge of Follow-through

Charles Kettering, the head of research at General Motors from 1920-1947, once said, "It is the 'follow through' that makes the great difference between ultimate success and failure, because it is so easy to stop."

Like many people, I have a standard practice of setting aside time to review the tsunami of emails that come in each day. To be most efficient, I try to touch each email only once. Upon opening the email, I make an immediate decision and take action: delete, save, respond, or forward. Once I have responded or forwarded the email to someone else, I figure that the ball is now in the recipient's court and nothing more is required of me until their next email.

Here's the problem: People miss emails. Emails sometimes

incorrectly get sent to spam folders. Responses sometimes end up in outgoing mail that gets blocked. More than once, I have failed to follow through on something that was important to me and missed an opportunity as a result. This was the result of an invisible agreement that I had with myself. It took a painful loss for me to become aware that I had a follow-through pattern in place that wasn't working and I needed a new, more intentional plan.

Businesses have many invisible agreements that get in the way of effective and purposeful follow-through, from not following through at all, to only following up when a crisis happens, to overdoing it and micromanaging the follow-up, which creates a raft of other issues.

There Is No Substitute for Working This out Together

There is no single right way to make or follow through on decisions. What works for one combination of people and circumstances may not work for another.

Whether your business is you alone or an organization of thousands, if you want to perform at your highest level, you must consciously work out how you will make, communicate, and follow through on decisions—and continue to work this process out as conditions and people change.

As president George W. Bush once said, "If this were a dictatorship, it'd be a heck of a lot easier." But this old-school idea that the boss decides and tells workers what to do doesn't work anymore, and probably never worked as well as people thought in the first place.

Many executives long for the perceived ease of command-

and-control. They are frustrated when employees don't act on their decisions. I frequently hear executives say, "I'm paying them," or, "They are lucky to have the job," or, "It's their job to do what I say." And all this may be true.

But is the point to be obeyed or to be successful?

Imagine someone making a decision that affects you without considering or discussing your capabilities, time, knowledge, or skills. Imagine being expected to follow through without being given context or the full information you needed. That would make your job a lot harder, wouldn't it? Yet that's what managers do to employees and colleagues by not involving them in the decision-making process.

Solving this problem is easy, and yet few managers have the awareness or the skills to do so. The first step in letting go of the old command-control mindset is to begin valuing the input and full involvement of others. This is the only way to ensure that everyone is playing the same game by the same rules.

Note: Agreement Does Not Equal Consensus

Consensus decision-making is rarely effective; it also rarely represents a true consensus. Coming to an agreement about how decisions will be made is not the same as having everyone in complete agreement with every decision. If that were the case, no decisions would ever get made. Agreement is more important regarding *how* decisions will be made than any individual decision itself.

There will be times when it is appropriate for a leader to make a unilateral decision. There will be times when not everyone affected will agree with a decision. This can all be worked through seamlessly when there is a clear agreement in the organization about the circumstances, reasons, and actions behind the decision-making process.

Apply the Second Agreement for Decision-Making Success

Remember the second agreement—how we will make it safe? Safety is the most essential ingredient for consistently effective decision-making. When people are afraid to make a wrong decision, they avoid making decisions. They slow-walk decisions. They over-research. They may play the game of Hot Potato, passing decision accountability from one person to another. Or they make fear-based decisions. (Ironically, "No" is almost always safer than "Yes," and decisions based on fear almost always set up the very situations they were designed to avoid.)

When fear is present, bad decisions—or no decisions at all—are made. Without decisions, there can be no forward movement. If it's not safe for people to make bad decisions, sometimes people won't be able to make good decisions either.

What does the safety to decide look like? It is a shift in perspective—a fundamentally different way of being.

With the team I am part of at IMPAQ, there is mutual shared understanding, acceptance, expectation, and support that we can count on all team members to make decisions that are as consistent as possible with our agreed-upon picture of success. We talk about how we will make decisions. We allow the time necessary for making decisions and assign leads to ensure forward movement. We schedule follow-ups. We take each other into consideration, consult each other, and make ourselves available to be consulted. When decisions turn out as expected, we celebrate them. When they don't, we celebrate that as well. We learn and adapt. We consciously avoid blame, judgment, or punishment. I have never felt so empowered, supported, committed to a shared outcome, or to my other team members as I do as a part of this team.

Decisions set implementation in motion. Implementation requires coordination. That's what's next.

Create a Visible Agreement about How You Will Make and Follow Through on Decisions

Agree on how the team will:

- Make it safe to decide
- Ensure decisions are aligned with mission, desired outcomes, and values
- Handle different types of decisions
- Involve the right people at the right times
- Consult each other
- Balance the needs for analysis, accuracy, and urgency
- Minimize risk and maximize impact
- Deal with disagreements and conflicts
- Act as one after a decision is made
- Determine who owns the follow-through
- Respond when decisions go wrong

Unsuccessful people make decisions based on their current situations.

Successful people make decisions based on where they want to be.

—Unknown

The Seventh Agreement: How We Will Share Information and Coordinate Actions

▶ THE NEW RULE ◀
THERE IS NO SUBSTITUTE FOR WORKING OUT HOW YOU WILL WORK TOGETHER

For years, Dr. Judy had been dreaming of a device that would make it easier for her patients to follow her medical advice at home. At long last, the state of technology made it possible, and Judy decided to leave her medical practice to open a med-tech startup. She knew she was racing the clock; that if she didn't get her product to market quickly, someone else would. Judy guarded her intellectual property zealously, even inside the company.

In the early days when there were just a few employees, this was easy, but after a few rounds of investment, the company had grown significantly. Judy felt strongly that information should be shared on a need-to-know basis. And in her opinion, most people simply did not need to know. When people started out, she would provide the necessary information on a just-in-time basis—sometimes even later than that.

Some departments had better access to information than others.

Some managers shared more with their teams than others. This led to confusion and resentment. Team members were frequently frozen, awaiting input from Judy or others.

Department leaders in the company often didn't have a full understanding of context, which meant they were unaware of information that could affect their department's ability to perform. They certainly didn't know what other departments were doing, and therefore couldn't possibly understand their needs.

The culture balkanized. Departments were actively hostile to each other and fiercely protective of their own ideas, efforts, and output. They did not value the contributions of others. They took actions that duplicated and/or counteracted those of other departments. To borrow a cliché, the right hand didn't know what the left was doing.

Judy was right about one thing: in a fast-moving industry, speed to market is the difference between success and failure. And nothing slows down speed to market like a failure to effectively coordinate. Lack of information flow set up poor decision-making as well as stalls and slowdowns in virtually every department. It took time for people to sort out what had been done and what needed to be undone. Each delay quickly grew exponentially because each department's slowdowns affected other departments. Product release was put off again and again. Key people became frustrated and left to take jobs with the competition. Several disgruntled employees sued the organization, leading to more distractions and a drain on essential resources.

In the end, competitive products did beat them to market.

Judy had recruited the world's best scientists to realize her vision, but without effective coordination, it didn't matter.

Coordination is the lifeblood of business. We need a smooth flow of information and ideas. We need to synchronize our efforts. Focus, productivity, collaboration, and growth are the results of clearly agreeing upon the process of working as a team. A lack of coordination can be fatal.

Failure to Share Information and Actions Is a Big Set-Up

Effective coordination doesn't happen by accident. If people and teams do not work out information flow and the actions they take, businesses face cascading bottom-line effects:

- Failure to meet deadlines and accomplish goals
- Poor decisions based on incorrect assumptions and out-of-date or partial information
- Inability to move forward
- Inadequate resolution of mission-critical problems
- Ineffective leveraging of opportunities, resources, knowledge, ability, and time
- Drama, distractions, employee turnover
- Inability to innovate effectively
- Attrition of both clients and talent
- Direct impact on revenues and profit margins

Symptoms of Dysfunctional Coordination

Brian sits on the advisory board for a large nonprofit organization that was experiencing operational and financial upheaval. Board membership had historically been honorary, with little actual involvement in the nonprofit's operation. During semiannual board meetings, people got together for courtesy updates and social interaction. As the nonprofit's struggles became more significant, the executive director stepped down. Board members became concerned and felt a responsibility to become more involved. The problem was that there was no habit of coordination between them. Each member had his or her own opinions about how the organization should proceed, but there was no protocol for coordinating their efforts. As this became clear, rather than working together, individuals began taking their own—often opposing—actions outside of the purview of the group.

You may recognize some of the symptoms they experienced, which frequently occur when there is a lack of coordination within an organization.

Factions formed and became gossip mills. Information was shared selectively, leaving out key people or important data. Some board members attempted to seize power and control. Others pushed for delay and decreased involvement. Conflict erupted. Misinformation spread. The nonprofit's reputation was damaged. People began assigning blame to each other and organization staff. This created mistrust, disengagement, resentment, and turnover. No forward movement was possible.

It's natural to get caught in the trap of blaming people for unproductive behaviors. But when we attribute these common patterns to people being incompetent, petty, power-hungry, unprofessional, or uncommitted, we miss the point. The absence of a clear cultural agreement about how we coordinate sets people up to behave in these ways and sets the organization up for failure.

Why People Resist Coordinating

Brian tried to get the board to work together. He proposed a meeting to get on the same page. No one accepted. Why not? They perceived the call for coordination as something that could result in having to give up the autonomy, power, and control to which they had become accustomed. Coming together might mean having to reveal actions they'd already taken which they knew were in opposition to other board members' opinions. Frankly, they didn't want face-to-face disagreement. So, instead, they chose passive disagreement behind each others' backs.

Early in my first career in advertising, I learned that creative directors and my creative colleagues could be swiftly brutal in knocking down nonconforming ideas—as well as the people who produced them. They were quick to label those with different sensibilities as "hacks." This impacted people's reputations, the quality of work assigned to them, and their ability to land work—not to mention their self-confidence. The risk of presenting a concept that deviated from the group sensibility was potentially career-ending.

I self-edited many creative ideas rather than take that risk. I'm not saying that all my ideas were brilliant, or even any good. But fear kept me from putting them out there. Chances are good that I killed some truly innovative concepts.

Most of us have had the experience of having our ideas ridiculed, or having someone else take credit for ideas we initiated. We have all been in situations in which information we needed was withheld, or information was used against us, or sharing information resulted in getting a smaller piece of the pie. These are painful experiences that can make us determined never to experience them again. Most people develop a set of inner beliefs about sharing information with others as a result. Generally, these beliefs are reactive and inconsistent with business success.

Secretive, self-protective behaviors, even if they were adopted with good reason at one time, have no place in a high-performing business. The only way for an organization to perform at its highest level is with open, timely, and intentional sharing and coordination. The only way to create the safety for effective coordination to happen is through mutual agreement.

The Impact of Perceived Time on Coordination

In the FreshBiz business simulation game that I facilitate for my clients, just as in real world business, there is a time crunch. Because players need to accomplish the objectives of the game within ninety minutes, they try to solve the game's problems on their own; it seems most expedient.

Game play demonstrates that coordinating with teammates

(instead of seeing them as competitors) always opens up tools, knowledge, and new possibilities that result in new strategies and rapid forward movement. In the debrief, we identify areas in the business where this same principle is at work—where coordination can make all the difference.

What Coordination Makes Possible

- Engagement
- Collaboration
- Mutual respect and trust
- Powerful decisions and solutions
- Improved response time and nimbleness
- Seeing and seizing opportunities
- Learning
- Much more

What it Looks Like: Questions to Explore Together

As you establish a shared organizational agreement to facilitate effective coordination, here are some of the most important discussion points:

- **What is our intention?** When people share information and ideas, or coordinate efforts, they need to know why they are doing so and what results they want to come out of the coordination—and they need to communicate that intention.

- **When will we coordinate?** What does timely mean for your company? What kinds of circumstances indicate immediate sharing or coordination?

- **Who needs to be in the loop?** Who is affected by information and ideas? Who can contribute? How will you involve people? What and how will you communicate with others?

- **How much will we share?** Are team members sharing enough information with each other, or dumping too much? How much information is optimal for which circumstances?

- **How will we coordinate?** When is a meeting most appropriate versus a phone call or an email?

- **How will team members respond?** How will you make it safe for team members to express their needs? How will you encourage healthy mutual support?

- **What information needs to be held in confidence?** And what does that mean in your organization?

- **How will we deal with broken coordination?** People are human. They will overdo, underdo, and blurt things out that they shouldn't have. If your team expects such things and knows what to do when they happen, you can course-correct quickly and skip the breakdowns and drama.

- **What will you reward and encourage—and how?** Any behaviors you want to continue, you need to acknowledge—consistently. Get on the same page with this. And ask yourselves, "Where are we, perhaps unintentionally, discouraging the coordination we want?"

No matter how effectively you do coordinate, people are human, the unexpected will happen and problems will arise. Next up, how to be prepared for them.

Create a Visible Agreement about How You Will Coordinate

Agree on how the team will:

- Get clear on the intention regarding coordination of information and actions
- Determine when coordination is appropriate
- Involve the right people
- Communicate effectively
- Neither overshare nor undershare
- Deal with confidential information or sensitive actions
- Reward and encourage effective coordination
- Anticipate and respond to breakdowns
- Much more

If everyone is moving forward together then success takes care of itself.

—Henry Ford

The Eighth Agreement: How We Will Respond to Challenges

▶ THE NEW RULE ◀
PROBLEMS ARE YOUR TEACHERS

Frank was the head of a boutique film production company. He was admired both internally and across the community for producing unique, high-quality, creative work. Overall the company had a positive culture. They paid well and people wanted to work there. Ping-pong and pool tables in the common areas were always busy. People appreciated their fun company events. Frank was proud that his staff was happy.

For the most part, things went smoothly. Even in Frank's happy little business, however, people sometimes didn't do what they were supposed to do. Team members sometimes dropped the ball and failed to catch it before it became a client problem. Employees sometimes didn't share necessary information in time to prevent a minor crisis.

These issues didn't happen often, but when problems surfaced, Frank didn't know what to do. His fear of mishandling the situation caused him to delay taking any action at all. In such situations, Frank would avoid the person at the core of the issue and consult with multiple others about how to address it—partially looking for advice, but mostly hoping that someone else would deal with the problem. This behavior started a gossip mill, which would inevitably reach the person in question, creating upset and additional problems on top of the original issue—which still had not been addressed. Everyone in the company could feel the pressure increasing as Frank put off the inevitable. Finally, the situation would reach a crisis-point, Frank would blow up and yell out all the frustration he'd been withholding, and the team member would cry or walk out or otherwise react. And Frank would find himself apologizing for his own bad behavior and promising to do things differently. The focus would then fall on Frank instead of the unresolved issue. Everything would go back to normal for a while—until the issue surfaced again.

Can you spot the hidden agreement?

Business management author and guru Patrick Lencioni once said, "Most of the CEOs who fail think they will find the solution to their problems in finance, marketing, strategic planning, etc., but they don't look for the solution to their problems inside themselves."

Frank was the origin of his organization's dysfunction. But everyone in the company was involved in perpetuating the way the business dealt with problems.

I had been coaching Frank on and off for a year before I witnessed one of these situations first hand. We talked about what was getting in the way of handling problems as they arose.

Frank had bad memories of other leaders seriously botching

employee feedback and had seen this destroy the culture in companies he'd worked at in the past. He had the best of intentions: he did not want to make that same mistake, which was causing him to make a completely *different* set of mistakes.

Frank and I gathered the team and had a candid conversation about how they approached problems. It was a huge surprise—and relief—for Frank to hear that his team actually *wanted* feedback— especially when they were getting something wrong. This created an opening for a clear agreement regarding the best way people could approach each other when they were off track. We agreed on what the team could do if they noticed that Frank (or anyone) was not addressing an issue.

The Problem with Problems

The breakdowns in Frank's company generally started as soon as he labeled something a problem. We humans are very creative when we don't know how to deal with a problem. We find all kinds of ways to ignore it, deny that it is a problem, play the blame game, rationalize it, flat-out refuse to address it, and even go into hiding to avoid it. In his Personal Accountability Model (see Appendix), Mark Samuel calls these behaviors "The Victim Loop," because when we engage in any of these responses to a challenge, we remain stuck in the problem rather than moving toward a solution.

At the management level, behaviors that keep us from addressing problems cause team members to avoid identifying situations that need to be rectified. This tends to drive obstacles to success underground, where they can quietly take root and grow. Have you noticed how often things we label as problems don't go away, but instead become bigger?

Carl Jung said, "What you resist not only persists, but will grow in size." We have seen this over and over in the public arena. Between the time the United-States-led "War on Terror" was launched (after September 11, 2001) and 2013, global terrorism fatalities actually increased fivefold.[24] Likewise, the "war on drugs" has only strengthened the illicit drug market.[25] And despite the ubiquitous American war against obesity, our population becomes heavier every year.[26]

Consider the possibility that no problem is real; any problem is merely a perception. In reality, there are only situations and circumstances—the way things are. Your business can label circumstances "problems," or it can label them "opportunities." How your team frames situations has a profound influence over your ability to move forward. The use of the word "problem" sets us up to see situations in a limited way and to get trapped in The Victim Loop. So, the first part of any organizational agreement for effectively identifying and solving problems needs to address how you see, talk about, and treat challenges.

Perhaps psychologist Theodore Isaac Rubin said it best: "The

---

[24] Gilsinan, Kathy. "The Geography of Terrorism." *The Atlantic.* November 18, 2014. https://www.theatlantic.com/international/archive/2014/11/the-geography-of-terrorism/382915/, referencing the "Global Terrorism Index 2014" report by The Institute for Economics and Peace. http://visionofhumanity.org/app/uploads/2017/04/Global-Terrorism-Index-Report-2014.pdf.

[25] Friedersdorf, Conor. "America Has a Black-Market Problem, Not a Drug Problem." *The Atlantic.* March 17, 2014. https://www.theatlantic.com/politics/archive/2014/03/america-has-a-black-market-problem-not-a-drug-problem/284447/, referencing an Associated Press quote by General John F. Kelly, testifying before the Senate Armed Services Committee.

[26] Murray, Christopher J.L. and Ng, Marie. "Nearly One-Third of the World's Population is Obese or Overweight, New Data Shows." Institute for Health Metrics and Evaluation, May 2014.

problem is not that there are problems. The problem is expecting otherwise and thinking that having problems is a problem."

Agree to Surface Obstacles and Challenges

When challenges arise, if we get caught in The Victim Loop and ignore, deny, blame, rationalize, resist, or hide from them, we set up a delay in addressing them that will create gaps in performance. The longer the delay, the bigger the gaps and the greater the costs. Eventually, unaddressed challenges will lead to a crisis that will finally reveal the truth of the situation, and no matter how painful or embarrassing, this is a blessing in disguise. A crisis wakes people up, making possible the conversations, teamwork, and actions needed to create improvement.

High-performance teams know that this is the most inefficient way to operate. They recognize the importance of surfacing and solving problems as they go.

In her 2014 Harvard Graduate School of Education TEDx talk, Harvard Business School professor of leadership and management Amy Edmondson refers to research in which she studied medication errors in two hospitals. The study's question: "Do better teams make fewer mistakes?" Her data showed that exactly the opposite was true. Better teams were making more mistakes, not fewer!

Edmondson realized that better teams were, in fact, not actually more error-prone. Rather, they were more willing to acknowledge and discuss their mistakes. They had created a climate of openness that allowed and encouraged them to report and address challenges.

What This Agreement Looks Like

It seems obvious that willingness to accept and talk about what is *not* working leads to catching and correcting mistakes and gaps earlier, thus minimizing the size and seriousness of any repercussions.

To perform at its highest level, your team needs to agree about what you need to put in place so people can identify what is happening and address it as early as possible. This means instead of engaging in the behaviors of The Victim Loop, you'll want to agree to engage in the behaviors that my IMPAQ colleagues and I call The Accountability Loop:

- **Acknowledge the Truth of the Situation**

  How can you possibly make good decisions, provide quality customer service, maintain a trusted reputation in the marketplace, and retain client, vendor, and internal relationships if you are trading in denials, distortions, or flat-out lies? The truth is reality, and as my first coach used to tell me, *reality wins—but only one hundred percent of the time.*

  And yet, people in business regularly deal in untruths and partial truths, especially where problems are concerned. Often, these decisions are not based in malice—just people's efforts to not upset others or themselves and to look as good as possible.

  The high-performing team doesn't allow or encourage such deflection. When you create your organizational agreement about how you will seamlessly flag and solve problems, it is critical that you agree to deal in and with the truth, for better or worse.

- **Own the Situation and Its Outcomes**

  In his book, *Making Yourself Indispensable: The Power of Personal Accountability*, Mark Samuel says, "When you own something you are more likely to take care of it. You are more likely to feel responsible for it."[27] Everyone involved owns their experience of a problem, as well as their experience of resulting outcomes—or the solution. Samuel goes on to say, "We don't just own the problems we create. We own the ones that we promote through our communication and attitude. And we own the problems that we allow to exist and do nothing about."

  When people in your organization agree to take on this kind of ownership, you get greater engagement, better solutions, better follow-through, and significantly fewer of the behaviors that perpetuate problems.

- **Forgive Others, Circumstances, and Yourself**

  Blame is one of the most natural—and unhelpful—responses to obstacles. Blaming others, the situation, or even ourselves never provides a solution. It only blocks the creative thinking that could get us out of whatever mess we are in.

---

[27] Samuel, Mark. *Making Yourself Indispensable: The Power of Personal Accountability.* New York: Portfolio/Penguin, 2012.

Agree to drop blame and judgment. Forgive people for making mistakes; forgive situations for going wrong; forgive ourselves for things we did or didn't do or think.

This doesn't mean allowing what isn't working to continue.

When my daughter's club volleyball team missed a shot, they had a practice of high-fiving. This was a way of forgiving the miss. Anything else would have kept them stuck in the former play and unable to be fully present for the next play.

Allowing team members to miss a shot and know they were good to go on to the next one without blame or judgment is essential for forward movement. And forward movement is essential for business success.

- **Ask Good Questions**

   Problems don't just happen. They come into being as a result of previous thinking and actions. To move your organization to a better place in the face of a problem, you'll need an agreement in place that allows your team to explore the circumstances, what happened that led you to this place, and what you might do differently now. Here are a few good questions to start with:

   - **Is the source of the problem internal or external?**
      Make sure that you are addressing what is within your control and acknowledging what is not.

- **Is the breakdown rooted in process or performance?** If people are underperforming—why? It could be that a process needs adjustment. Or perhaps team members are missing knowledge or skills, need training, or aren't a good fit for the job. Expectations may not be clear. Management may be failing to communicate and/or hold people accountable. Identifying the root cause will support the most effective response.

- **Is the issue one of practicality or safety?** Consider whether expectations are reasonable and possible. Look at whether the problem may be caused by too much risk to take the necessary actions.

- **Is it a problem of creativity or capability?** Creativity can compensate for many kinds of lack. But when creativity isn't working, capabilities may need to be expanded.

- **Are conflicting priorities getting in the way?** Sometimes one task or responsibility precludes another. Generally, these need to be solved by leaders a level or two above the presenting challenge, where priorities are set and managed.

- **What are the costs of the problem?** Knowing what the problem is costing the company, financially and otherwise—as well as the costs associated with no change—can be a useful guide to actions and speed required.

- **Are conflicting personalities the issue?** Many leaders are tempted to ignore interpersonal conflicts. Even when issues seem strictly personal, they are critical to address ASAP. Over time, unresolved conflicts become harder and harder to resolve and can cascade into larger and irreconcilable differences. Get people in conflict to change direction as early as possible. Get intervention. There are consultants who specialize in this field.

- **Learn**

    Every problem offers a hidden gift: learning. If you are open to it, problems teach your team what is not working and what might work better. When we see problems as opportunities to learn and improve, problems actually empower organizations.

- **Take Action**

    It's quite easy to become frozen when confronted with problems. It can be tempting to analyze, to want to come up with the perfect plan, or to postpone doing anything until you are certain that the problem will be solved.

    Of course, such certainty is impossible. While you are analyzing, the performance gap is widening. An essential part of a healthy organizational agreement to deal effectively with challenges is taking action, based on the above thinking, so you can continue to learn and adjust.

Proactive Recovery Is the Name of the Game

When confronted with allegations of sexual harrassment in his organization, Travis Kalanick, the cofounder and former CEO of ridesharing service company Uber, reacted by ignoring the problem, denying his part in the problem, and publicly blaming other employees. His behaviors created a cascade of increasingly bigger problems that cost the company hundreds of thousands of customers, a lawsuit, and ultimately led to his resignation. At its peak, private markets valued Uber at $70 billion. These problems caused a drop in market value of more than $20 billion. The organization's failure to quickly and effectively acknowledge and address these challenges cost nearly one-third of the company's value.

Although most businesses don't experience it in such a spectacular fashion, many unconsciously turn what could be small problems into much larger ones because they are unprepared and react inappropriately. Reacting to problems almost always involves the victim behaviors outlined earlier.

The unexpected can easily throw a business off its game. Championship sports teams know this. They prepare for all kinds of possibilities, including the ones they *can't* anticipate. They know exactly what they will do to get back in the game no matter what happens.

Business leaders who want their organizations to perform at their highest level anticipate the various what-ifs and agree in advance on action plans to recover as quickly and seamlessly as possible when the unwanted happens.

We call this *recovery planning*. The idea is to have the courage to anticipate and acknowledge what might go wrong and discuss in advance how individuals and teams will respond. You can even agree ahead of time about what you will do if something you haven't anticipated happens.

Here are a few things to discuss together to get you started:

- **Who are the go-to people for different types of issues?** Team members need to know whom they can approach when problems arise. Look for the gaps and fill them.

- **How quickly will team members act and react when problems are identified?** Minimize the waste of time, but also allow time to find the root causes that might be causing repetitive or additional breakdowns.

- **How deep will you go?** Not every challenge requires root-cause investigation. Conversely, the costs of band-aid solutions to recurring problems can really add up. Agree to be conscious about how you will know when to dive deep.

- **Who gets consulted and when?** Identify how the team will determine who is involved and affected by a problem. Agree on the timing that will be most effective for involving others.

- **How will you determine who takes action and how they will follow up?** Decide in advance who owns next steps and how they will communicate resolution to the team.

- **How will you evaluate success?** If you don't have a clear picture of what success looks like, you may not know whether a solution truly addressed the problem.

Sometimes failure happens. How to turn it into success is up next.

Create a Visible Agreement for How Your Organization Will Respond to Challenges

Agree on how the team will:

- Remain conscious of how we think about and respond to problems
- Make it safe to identify challenges
- Acknowledge the truth of the situation
- Own the situation and the outcomes
- Ask good questions
- Learn
- Take action
- Anticipate what could go wrong and create recovery plans

Not everything that is faced can be changed.
But nothing can be changed until it is faced.

—James Baldwin

The Ninth Agreement:
How We Will Utilize Failure

► THE NEW RULE ◄
FAILURE IS NECESSARY FOR SUCCESS

Everything in Matt's experience had led him to believe in loyalty. Matt was the senior executive for the United States division of a global manufacturing company. He had landed the job right out of college and had never worked anywhere else. His was a real, old-fashioned employer-employee relationship story. The company had seen his value, promoted him again and again, and he had spent more than half of his forty-five-year life working within its walls. He prided himself on creating the same kind of experience for the people who worked for him. Together, they had come up with both product and process innovations that had produced nearly $80 million in revenues worldwide. Because Matt had been such a good team player, no one outside the company's walls knew how much value his division was providing.

Like many manufacturers, through the years the parent company had responded to economic pressures and moved more and more American manufacturing functions to Southeast Asia. Staff cuts had been unavoidable. Matt had been understanding when corporate reduced the headcount from 400 people to just about 300. He had let the weakest performers go, and that was probably for the best. He had been supportive when they downsized again to just over 200. But that one hurt; Matt had to cut people he cared about, who had given a significant part of their lives to making the company successful.

Now the parent organization was planning another staff reduction of nearly 100 people. He knew his top performers were preparing their resumes. He had already lost several young, emerging leaders to outside offers. Even if he was committed to saving his core team at all costs, these remaining employees were questioning whether this was a company with a future. And Matt felt like a failure because he had no idea how to change the global forces that were pushing on them. It looked like the division was failing them and failing, period.

Morale was sinking with each reduction. Fear was rising. Matt was doing what he always did: attempting to paint the most positive picture of the future. He could see people weren't buying it. Heck, he was having a harder and harder time believing it himself.

Their Invisible Agreements

Under Matt's leadership, failure simply wasn't acknowledged. Everyone knew to whitewash what was happening—to put a happy face on it. Their agreement was to loyally support whatever the parent company asked for, without complaint. The group ignored anything that looked like failure, aligned with corporate instructions, and disengaged from negative results. This had prevented them from taking actions that would have communicated their value to the company and allowed them to play a bigger game.

At this point, however, Matt could no longer deny the writing on the wall. Going along with the next cut would mean the end of the division. His loyalty to his people and the plant finally superseded his loyalty to the global corporation. He brought me in to assist with getting the team to see the situation clearly and figure out how they needed to reinvent themselves to survive. Together, they agreed not to fail. We devised a strategy for building global relationships to help company leaders understand that they could improve processes and cut costs significantly for the organization's facilities around the globe.

Once they did this, something amazing happened. Not only did Matt's group avoid that final cut, but their corporate parent also started investing more in their division. Suddenly they were playing a visible role in facilities all over the world. The cuts turned out to be an essential step in their growth—forcing Matt to seek assistance and begin to get clear about aligning the division's actions with their desired outcomes.

Other Invisible Agreements About Failure

Like Matt's, many organizations ignore warning signs and fail because of it. They excuse what's going on and rationalize it— sometimes until there is no business left.

Other leaders fear failure so much they see it in *everything*. They anticipate failure in situations in which they are actually succeeding. They over-scrutinize and overanalyze, unintentionally paralyzing themselves. Their efforts to avoid failure create problems, slowdowns, and breakdowns.

Some organizations blame and punish anything that smells like failure with the intention of stopping it in its tracks. Then there are those that are so embarrassed by the idea of failing that their invisible agreement is to hide mistakes and breakdowns—not only from the outside world, but also from themselves.

There are innumerable agreements that teams and organizations enter into unconsciously: driving people too hard, trying to force success, and making unrealistic promises. The list goes on and on.

Seven of the Many Ways Businesses Unintentionally Create Failure

- Ignore the situation
- Deny ownership of the problem
- Blame people and circumstances
- Rationalize and justify
- Jump from solution to solution
- Overanalyze
- Expect and fear failure

Fear of Failure Creates Failure

Have you ever been in a situation where you believed you were going to fail? I have, more than once.

The first time I experienced the FreshBiz business simulation, I played with three people I had never met before. One player only wanted to gamble; he lost and regained millions over and over again. Another player wanted to figure it out for himself—and by himself. The third player was passive and silent. I suggested that we collaborate. I suggested that we get coaching from the game's creator, who was in the room and offering support. The other players were adamant that they did *not* want to do this. One wanted to get back into the casino; the other didn't want help figuring it out; the third didn't speak up. Time was short. It was crystal clear to me that what we were doing was not working. But I didn't believe I had the time to convince them to play differently.

And so, I gave up.

I didn't quit the game, but in my mind, I decided that we were going to lose, and I stopped trying. I kept doing the same things that weren't working until the simulation ended.

Of course, we did lose.

A few days later, I was on the phone with a prospective client who was exhibiting the same kind of closed-off, blindered behavior as my teammates in the simulation. Because of the simulation experience, I heard myself thinking, "Forget it. This isn't going anywhere."

I was about to give up!

But then I remembered the simulation experience and I made a different decision. I changed my mindset and started asking different questions. I challenged the prospect. And I turned what would have been a failure into a success.

How many times had I failed in the past because I allowed the idea of failure to shut down my creativity? I'll never know.

Since then, I have facilitated other teams in creating turnarounds in the simulation that translate into turnarounds in their businesses. There were so many options available to me that first time, but I clung to the idea that there was no hope and didn't even see them.

People do this in business all the time.

A national advertising agency had the opportunity to buy an award-winning regional agency that had cultivated a sexy and viral brand image. Naturally, there were many competitors for the acquisition, leading to a bidding war. The senior leaders of the national firm, wanting to ensure their organization won, used their leverage and clout to seal the deal with less than their usual due diligence.

As things moved forward, it became clear that the agency they had acquired, while brilliant creatively, lacked business savvy. Serious financial problems that had been hidden began to surface. Those at the adoptive parent company developed the sinking feeling that they had bought a lemon.

From this perspective, the senior leadership team put pressure on their acquisition to solve its own problems; however, with no faith in their ability to do so, the new parent simultaneously cut the agency's resources. The senior leaders reluctantly supported the agency in some turnaround efforts, but each time, at the first hint of failure, they would pull the plug and send the acquired agency back to the drawing board.

These leaders mistook blame for accountability and thought they'd done something meaningful, even though there was no actual forward movement toward the desired outcome. As a result, the acquired agency team's frustration grew and their commitment quickly lessened.

After a while, the acquirer began to see their purchase as something to be dismantled for its component parts. They relocated key clients and talent to other offices. Within two years, they completely closed the doors, having destroyed what they had once set out to own.

As soon as they labeled the project a *failure*, creativity stopped. Fear of failure made the parent company create the very situation they wanted to avoid. They shut down not only their own creative thinking, but also creative thinking throughout the organization.

Naturally, fear of failure has predictable consequences. People become hesitant to risk and reluctant to try anything new, keeping the organization stuck with old practices that need updating. Team members become blind to opportunities right in front of their faces. Fear in one situation spreads to other situations. When organizations do this over and over again, they set up a culture of failure and don't even know they are creating it themselves. This pattern becomes entrenched in the organization's behaviors and in its reputation, both internally and externally. All this predictably affects the business's ability to attract and retain talent and clients, and ultimately to achieve its potential.

Like Problems, Failure Does Not Really Exist

Matt's tale (from the beginning of this chapter) of repeated downsizings and quiet desperation is not an anomaly. Look deeply at any success, and somewhere in the middle, it probably looked like failure. *Failure* is a story we tell ourselves when things aren't going as expected or desired. That perspective determines what we see as possible and how we respond. Under those same circumstances, we could also take the same information as constructive feedback, a sign that we need to adjust, problem-solve, learn, do something new and different, and look for the opportunity.

In business, it's critical to be prepared for those midcourse moments that feel like things are tanking. If you perceive setbacks as permanent failure, you are more likely to take action that ensures failure. But if you train yourself to hold perspectives that help you learn, shift, and keep moving forward, there is no such thing as failure.

Developing organizational trust that setbacks aren't the entire picture can change what is possible.

How you hold and deal with failure is something you need to do collectively. One person in an influential position with dysfunctional thinking and behaviors can derail an entire organization. This is why your business needs a shared agreement about how you will think, what you will do when it looks like the worst is happening, and how you will catch yourselves when thinking and behaviors are creating the very failures you are trying so desperately to avoid.

This doesn't mean that everyone will always handle failure perfectly. They won't. Having agreements in place gives the team a clear path to getting back on track quickly and seamlessly when difficulties threaten your picture of success.

Fear of Failure and Accountability Cannot Coexist

One of my favorite business books, *Creativity, Inc.* by Ed Catmull, founder and CEO of Pixar, holds a radical truth: "To be wrong as fast as you can is to sign up for aggressive rapid learning."[28]

This is accountable thinking; neither expecting that things will always go your way, nor ignoring, denying, excusing, or blaming when they don't. Accountability is all about staying committed to desired outcomes. Fear of failure is inconsistent with this commitment.

Can we agree that reality is messy? Setbacks will happen. It is an enormous waste of time to expect reality will not throw us challenges and curve balls. They come at us with a fury. The best response is to remain committed to the picture of success you created in Agreement Three. See breakdowns as learning opportunities and you will gain knowledge, skill, alignment and ultimately success. Malcolm Forbes once said, "Failure is success if you learn from it."

The only way to fail is to give up.

What's needed is a new mindset. How would your business be different if people weren't afraid? Would they innovate more? Solve problems faster? Would you see an increase in accountability for results?

One thing is certain: you won't produce the new results you want with fear-based thinking.

Agree to a Healthy Relationship with Failure

The first step toward maximum utilization of failure is to disconnect failure from blame—in fact, get rid of blame altogether. If team members believe that failure will reflect poorly on them—perhaps

---

[28] Catmull, Ed. *Creativity, Inc.: Overcoming the Unseen Forces that Stand in the Way of True Inspiration.* Random House, 2014.

enough to put their jobs in jeopardy—it will limit their ability to take needed action. Approaching failure with courage and without judgment is essential. Make an agreement that encourages people to tell and accept the truth of the situation. Develop better listening. Reframe failure as learning. Determine what it looks like in your company to be open-minded and forgiving. Agree on how to give each other feedback that will keep the business moving forward. Get shared clarity about how you will deal with setbacks when they inevitably arise.

What If Something Truly Isn't Working?

Avoiding a failure mindset does not mean ignoring what doesn't work. Acknowledge the truth of the situation, make necessary adjustments, and keep moving.

Sometimes you may need to substantially change or even shut down a project, initiative, product, service line, or an entire business. If you are operating based on the other agreements in this book, you will understand that a decision to end something is not a failure.

Let's also apply this thinking to people. Sometimes a person won't be a fit for a task, position, or even for the business overall. Labeling a person as a failure prevents the company from learning how to staff better and also prevents the person from moving on in the most positive way for everyone concerned.

Don't fool yourself into thinking that others in the organization aren't affected by the way you deal with their colleagues' failures. A team agreement helps the organization to recognize when someone is not performing and supports the entire organization in improving.

That agreement can also prepare the team to recognize when team members are not a fit and support them in finding their next fit with kindness.

You might have noticed the link between everything that we are talking about and accountability. Accountability is the master agreement and the final one; we'll discuss it in the next (and final) chapter.

Create a Visible Agreement About How You Will Utilize Failure

Agree on how the team will:

- Disconnect failure from blame
- Cultivate the courage and safety to look at the truth of the situation
- Agree to be open-minded and forgiving
- Develop better listening
- Reframe failures as learning opportunities
- Get shared clarity about how you will deal with setbacks
- Identify underperformance and provide support to improve
- Recognize when someone is not a fit and provide support to move on

Success is not final, failure is not fatal: it is the courage to continue that counts.

—Winston Churchill

The Tenth and Master Agreement: How We Will Become Accountable

▶ THE NEW RULE ◀
ALL THAT MATTERS IS ENSURING AGREED-UPON ACTIONS PRODUCE AGREED-UPON RESULTS

Even with plenty of prior experience, I couldn't believe how we'd been set up to fail. I'd been freelancing as a copywriter at a Los Angeles ad agency working on a prominent cable television account for about half a year. On each job, less and less information was provided, and we were given shorter and shorter timeframes in which we were expected to produce award-winning creative presentations.

On this particular day, Gil, the account executive, came in with the brief. Only two out of twelve information sections were completed: the offer and the promise to the client—a 2 percent increase in response. He handed the single page to my art director partner and to me and told us the client needed to see something the following day.

"What?" We asked, in unison. "With what input?"

"This is all we've got," shrugged Gil. "You'll just have to work without it."

Understand that each job meant creating multiple concepts,

getting them approved by the creative director (who never approved anything on the first round), developing layouts and copy, getting those approved by both creative and account management, sourcing artwork, interfacing with the production department to ensure that our ideas could be produced within the budget (which had not been provided), and preparing our presentation.

And we had other jobs on our plate with concurrent deadlines.

The minute Gil was out the door, my art director, Stan, took the page, crumpled it and banked a shot off the wall into the circular file. Two points.

"Will this be the one?" With each job, we wondered if this would be the time that we would fail to deliver. So far, we had always pulled something off. We started to make up our own input; after all we needed direction from somewhere. In the absence of client input, we could do whatever we wanted.

Years of similar exercises had prepped us to work fast. We cranked out a few ideas in the next hour and took them to the creative director. We went back for round two and sent the ideas that survived to production for estimates. I knocked out some fast copy and we roped a couple of junior creatives in to work on layouts. We had several fights with Gil over the size of the call to action and the logo. We brought in the creative director, who pulled rank and negotiated something that none of us were happy with. We turned our attention to the other projects scheduled to go out that day.

Proud of ourselves for the fastest ever project turnaround, we went off to the client with the work the next day. I took the lead on the creative presentation, did my setup, and revealed the ideas.

The clients stared at us in stunned silence.

"Where's the part about our award?" the head of marketing blurted.

It was our turn to be speechless.

It turned out that the client had mentioned to Gil that they wanted an ad that focused on an industry award they had just received. Gil, who believed the offer was everything, had disregarded that piece of information and failed to share it with us.

Embarrassed and angry, we went back to the drawing board, now focusing on how to give the client what they wanted to see. Any thought of what would be compelling to the end customer (and in the clients' best interests) was a distant memory.

We went back to the client the next day, where they grudgingly approved the new approach and it moved into production. Weeks later, the response didn't look good, so the account team delayed sharing results. And then they delayed again, and again. No one really noticed because we had all immediately moved on to the next rush project.

This basic pattern continued for two years, until the agency lost the account. The account team blamed the creative team. The creatives blamed the account team. And everyone blamed the client.

No one ever questioned that senior management held the account team responsible for sales numbers each month. They held the creative team accountable for producing creative work that won awards. And no one was held accountable for the big-picture client results, or even for agency results.

No one in this entire scenario was held meaningfully accountable, myself included.

What Does It Mean to Be Accountable?

People in business talk about accountability a lot. They talk about *holding people accountable*, by which they generally mean, "Who can we blame?" They talk about *taking accountability*, by which they seem to mean "accepting blame." They talk about *being accountable*, by which they usually seem to mean "doing what you say you will do."

Dictionaries define accountable as some version of, "*Subject to giving an account: answerable; held accountable for the damage.*"

This definition is useless in the business world, because its focus is after the fact. It implies blame, perhaps regarding repayment or cleanup of a mess. But if accountability only kicks in once a failure has occurred, after the damage is done, it cannot support a business in reaching its goals and objectives.

Blame, no matter where it is directed, no matter how much (misguided) satisfaction it produces, does not move us toward outcomes. Even doing what we say we will do is no guarantee that we will produce results. None of these things help us to accomplish the outcome that lacked accountability. So even when we "hold people accountable," we are not being accountable for the outcomes.

We need a better, more actionable definition of accountability. And my partner, Mark Samuel, of IMPAQ Corporation, has created the best one I've seen:

> *Organizational or team accountability is the ability to count on each other to take action that is consistent with agreed-upon desired outcomes.*

There are actually four big essential ideas contained within this simple, elegant sentence.

1. Accountability is about outcomes.
2. Agreement on the desired outcomes is essential to be accountable.
3. Action that is consistent with the desired outcomes is the measure of accountability.
4. Accountability is dependent on interconnection and trust between people.

True accountability requires shared commitment to taking actions that produce the organization's desired results. Any mindset or action that is not consistent with the outcome you want is not accountable. Period.

Anything else is a hidden game—and it's playing you.

Why Accountability Is the Master Agreement

Agreeing to be accountable begins with a shared value for true accountability, and a shared effort to let go of old, ineffective ideas about accountability. Becoming accountable is an agreement to drop the blame game and to support each other in creating a culture of commitment to desired outcomes. It's an agreement to create the safety to acknowledge the truth of situations without judgment. It's an agreement to allow people to be imperfect, as long as we recognize reality and support each other in getting back on track.

Organizational accountability encompasses all the agreements we've discussed so far. This is why it is the master agreement. Being accountable depends on having agreements in place about:

- How we talk about the business
- How we make it safe to succeed
- Aligning behind a clear picture of success
- Who does what—and how we interconnect
- Where we put our attention
- How we make and follow through on decisions
- How we coordinate information and actions
- How we respond to challenges
- How we utilize failure

Accountability encompasses *all* the necessary agreements. You'll know what those agreements need to be by becoming aware of the pain points, slowdowns, and breakdowns in day-to-day execution.

Conscious awareness and the courage to address what is real in your business are the gateway to accountability.

The only way to be accountable is through clarity, and the only way to collectively become clear is to come into agreement. The only way to come into agreement is to work it out together. The ten agreements in this book are by no means all the agreements needed for organizational success. They are the merely the ones I have identified as most foundational and universal.

It is most important not just to agree that you will do these things, but also to agree as to *how*. Your *how* will be unique to your organization. No other organization's *how* will be a perfect fit for your business. There is no substitute for working agreements out together—and for continuing to work them out as people and circumstances change.

We Play Many Hidden Games Around Accountability

Hidden games are played based on old ideas. We learned about accountability when we were young—in our first work experiences, and before that, in school, and even before that, in our families. We tend to unconsciously bring those well-intended but false definitions of accountability into our present situations and pay them forward to future generations. Playing by old rules feels like the right thing to do because it's what we've always seen others do. So, we unwittingly perpetuate a variety of hidden games that we can never win.

Here are a few of those hidden games to watch for:

- **The Blame Game:** We're all too familiar with this one. The invisible agreement in this game is that as long as someone is blamed, shamed, made to apologize, or pay, then accountability is in place. It isn't.

- **The It's-Not-Our-Fault Game:** This agreement is a variation on the blame game, because if we agree it's not our fault, we agree that there *is* fault, and it resides with people or circumstances beyond our control. This basically takes the team out of the game, with the assumption of powerlessness.

"It's not our fault" too often equals, "There is nothing we can do," and that equals inaction. This results in remaining stuck exactly where we are.

- **The Ignore Game:** This game is built on the shared agreement that we ignore information and don't deal with situations until they become crises. The result of this game is a hidden agreement to be putting out fires—continuously.

- **The Fear Game:** This is an agreement to allow what *might* go wrong to govern our thinking and actions.

- **The I'll-Do-it-Myself Game:** The invisible agreement in this victim game is, "No one can do it like I can." It might not sound like an agreement, but anyone who continues to participate in this game is actually in agreement with it, no matter how much they don't like it.

- **The Lack-of-Clarity Game:** In this challenging game, players agree to move forward without really knowing what they—or anyone else—are doing, or what outcomes they are trying to create. They implicitly agree that urgency is more important than results. This game usually depends on the invisible agreement, "We would rather assume than discuss," in which team members assume conditions, clarity, understanding, action, and results.

- **The Poor-Communication Game:** There are many ways to play this hidden game. The varied invisible agreements include "We don't provide full information," "We don't ask when we are missing something," "We don't share expectations," "We don't let others know when they have met, exceeded, or failed to meet expectations," "We don't acknowledge problems until we absolutely have to," and many others.

- **The Accountable-to-the-Wrong-Thing-Game:** In this game, people implicitly agree to take action that is consistent with something that is in opposition to the desired outcomes of the organization. For example, we might all agree that being kind and caring is our desired outcome. Kindness and caring are good. However, taken to an extreme and combined with The Ignore Game, they can lead to a lack of accountability for results.

The Accountability Game Is All about Execution

What is execution? According to accountability expert Mark Samuel, in his book *Creating the Accountable Organization,* "Performance execution is comprised of *habits* that represent the automatic behavior demonstrated on a consistent basis in the organization." He goes on to say, "Just as it is critical for a football team to determine the kind of performance execution—to be a passing team or a running team—necessary to win ball games, organizations need to determine the ideal habits of performance execution to achieve optimal business results."[29]

These habits are not merely individual ones. They are collective. Optimal team results cannot happen if team members can't count

---

[29] Samuel, Mark. *Creating the Accountable Organization,* op cit.

on each others' commitment to these shared habits. This is what the IMPAQ approach creates. We literally build an organization in which people can count on each other.

That is the heart of accountability.

Accountability Means New Habits

When people aren't accountable for desired outcomes, there is no reason to think critically, question assumptions, or put ourselves out to do things differently. As a result, we miss deadlines and overreach budgets. We drop the ball and fail to provide our best client service. We let each other down and destroy the trust between us. We cannot only be committed to accountability when it is convenient. That equals not being accountable.

"We can have the best strategy, perfect priorities, great systems, and if nobody is taking action toward the outcomes, or behaving in a way that complies with those systems, we won't get the result," says Annie Pratt, CEO of IMPAQ Entrepreneur, "So that is why habits, both individual and collective, are important."

Habit change cannot happen without mindset change. This means that developing new thinking is the prerequisite for accountability. So, what are the components of an accountable mindset?

- **Seeking Clarity.** Without clarity, we can't know when we have achieved our goals, accomplished our outcomes, or even if we're on the right track. Seeking clarity makes communication work, allays fears, and creates alignment.

- **Open Curiosity.** Most of the dysfunctional games above close off possibilities. The best antidote is open curiosity. When we cultivate an interest in *how* things work and *how* we can improve, we automatically stop playing to lose and start playing a bigger game.

- **Creativity.** We need new, creative ideas, and we need to develop our creative muscles to reliably produce them.

- **Collaboration.** Organizations were created so groups of people could become more than the sum of the individuals. This can only happen when we join together in purpose and action.

- **Taking Action.** There is a particular mindset that creates powerful action. It begins with the idea that action is desirable. We can't move forward without it. We can't learn without it.

- **Growth Mindset.** Looking at everything through the growth lens is what keeps organizations accountable for staying up-to-pace with the rapidly changing world around us.

Ensure Accountability with Measurement and Acknowledgment

You would never think that Brandy, a seminal figure in the public relations field, had a moment of doubt. She exuded confidence, and her firm was always the leader in their market. However, after the fifth turnover in less than four years in a key business development role in her company, Brandy reached out to me.

"I don't know why we can't get this right. Are there no qualified candidates out there?"

"What does success look like for someone in this role?" I asked.

"Bringing in business," she snapped, as if it should be obvious.

"I hear you," I said. "But that's not very specific. What are the metrics that good business development people in your field need to hit that result in business? How many meetings do they need to take each month? How many articles do they need to send out? How many touches does it take with each prospect to get to a transaction?"

"I don't know," Brandy replied. "That's their job."

Brandy's lack of clarity with each person who'd passed through the revolving door of business development in her firm had already cost the company at least $600,000 in search and salary, not counting lost opportunity costs.

Metrics are powerful tools and an essential aspect of accountability. How could Brandy or her business development people possibly be accountable for a desired outcome when they didn't have a specific, agreed-upon idea about what they were shooting for?

Waiting for the failure before accountability kicks in is far too late in the process. If Brandy and any of the employees who had rotated through her company had established some clear leading indicators, Brandy could have used that information to make better subsequent hires, identified the gap between reality and expectations early, and provided coaching or other support to get that function back on track. Chances are much better that she would have had a seasoned, fifth-year producer in place, instead of starting over once again.

Metrics, when used accountably, create clear expectations and allow everyone to gauge how things are going long before it's too late. Part of using metrics well lies in the understanding that "how we will measure success" is an agreement. Too often, metrics are forced on people and used in a punishing way. Metrics can create fear and stall-out or create safety and progress, depending on how you use them.

When they are offered in the spirit of support, most people welcome metrics and other constructive feedback. Both positive and constructive feedback are important tools for bringing people into accountability.

When asked to tell employees what they are doing right, managers frequently say, "Why should I have to be a cheerleader? People shouldn't need a lot of rah-rah just for doing their jobs."

They are missing the point. High-performing companies have clear mutual understandings about how they will provide feedback and acknowledgment. They know that people need feedback, not just about what they are doing wrong and what to do differently; they also need to know what to continue doing. If we don't communicate what people are doing well, they may miss the importance of those actions.

Whatever gets the most airtime is experienced as what is most important. Assuming that people know what they are doing well is not accountable management.

One manufacturing company I worked with many years ago acknowledged success by gathering the entire company in a multipurpose room. They would bring people to the front of the room and proclaim their successes, followed by singing a goofy "For-He's-A-Jolly-Good-Fellow" type song. The very shy director of engineering got one look at this and decided he did not *ever* want this to happen to him. For years, he ensured that his performance never reached the level where he might be acknowledged publicly in this way.

What is a reward for one person might be a punishment to another. Being accountable may mean letting go of traditions, shoulds, and our own preferences to work out agreements that produce optimal performance.

Accountability is a Collective Journey

Every business seeks results that can only be accomplished collectively. The whole reason for businesses to exist is to leverage the knowledge, skills, talents, and efforts of multiple people to produce a result that is bigger than any one person could produce on his or her own. Even if every team member is individually accountable, without creating alignment and accountability *among* people and teams and departments and divisions, organizations cannot achieve the coordination and collaboration they need to deliver on their mission.

To create alignment and coordination, there must be agreement.

Playing an accountable game is not for the faint of heart. Risk is required. We need to develop the ability and context to look at what we are doing that isn't working, as well as what we haven't been doing that perhaps would have produced better or faster results.

We need to be able to put aside pride, embarrassment, and

judgments to take a clear, objective look at where we are relative to where we need to be.

We need to let go of the fears that keep us from acting or speaking up.

We need to be willing to say things that haven't been said before and that, perhaps, no one else has been willing to voice.

We need to trust each other, even though we have been disappointed in the past.

We need to be vulnerable with others and ourselves, because invulnerability prevents accountability and gets in the way of execution.

We need to create these agreements, because nothing else is accountable.

Create a Visible Agreement about Becoming Accountable

Agree on how the team will:

- Talk about the business
- Create psychological safety
- Commit to a clear picture of success
- Prioritize your focus
- Determine who does what and how you depend on each other
- Decide and follow through
- Coordinate actions and information-sharing
- Respond to challenges
- Powerfully utilize failure
- Hold yourselves and each other accountable for taking actions that are consistent with all the above

Accountability separates the wishers in life from the action-takers that care enough about their future to account for their daily actions.

—John Di Lemme, Motivational Speaker

APPENDIX

Appendix A

THE IMPAQ PERSONAL ACCOUNTABILITY MODEL

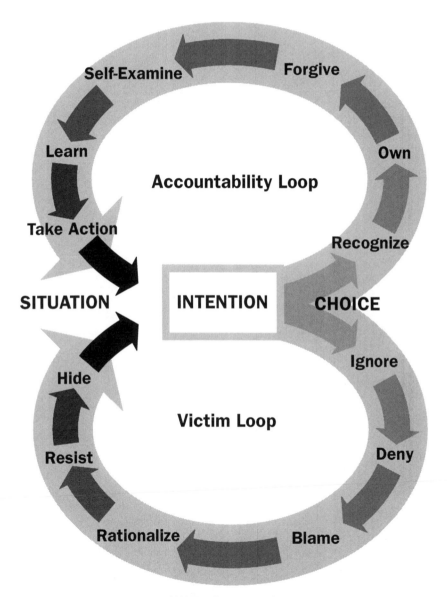

Self-Examine   **Forgive**

Learn   **Own**

Accountability Loop

Take Action   **Recognize**

SITUATION   **INTENTION**   **CHOICE**

Ignore

Hide

Victim Loop

Resist   **Deny**

Rationalize   **Blame**

Appendix B

FRESHBIZ: SPOT THE HIDDEN GAME IN YOUR ORGANIZATION

As I said in the first chapter, every business has a hidden game. And it's unlikely you'll be able to play a bigger, more successful game until you are aware of the games currently being played in your business that may be blocking you from reaching your potential.

That's where FreshBiz comes in. FreshBiz is a transformational three-hour experience that not only increases awareness of the thinking and behaviors that may be limiting your organization's growth, but also provides experiential learning—and practice—with the new thinking and collaborations that make new success possible.

- Would it make a difference in your organization if people and teams could better navigate the complexity of your business?

- What if, working together, your people could raise their performance, respond faster, and better spot and leverage opportunities?

- Would it improve efficiency if they were able to share information and coordinate their actions more smoothly?

- And what would be the impact of people getting out of their silos, and instead, keeping their focus on the big-picture objectives of the organization?

The FreshBiz experience provides big, Aha! moments on all of the above.

More than 50,000 business people in twenty-five countries are thinking and working more entrepreneurially because they experienced FreshBiz.

IBM, HP, Pfizer, L'Oreal, McCann Worldwide, WeWork, HSBC and even the United Nations are just a few of the recognizable organizations that have leveraged the FreshBiz experience to transform thinking, behaviors, and results.

This is why FreshBiz has been named a GameChangers 500 company: one of the 500 most game-changing businesses in the world, in the good company of Google, Zappos, Etsy, Toms, and others.

To get a demo, learn what happens at a FreshBiz workshop, and explore how FreshBiz could support growth in your organization, email sharon@thinkbusinessgrowth.com.

Appendix C

THINK BUSINESS GROWTH: SUPPORT FOR RAPID ORGANIZATIONAL CHANGE

Thank you for reading *Your Hidden Game*. I wrote this book to share some of the transformational ideas that have changed my life, my business, and the lives and businesses of dozens of my clients. You may be wondering about the work my clients and I do together.

My clients are leaders in their industries. They formed their organizations to make a difference. And they know that to accomplish their mission they need high-performance leadership, execution, and accountability at every level of their organizations. To realize their visions, they need staff to undertake a higher level of teamwork, both within and across functions. They need relationships inside and outside the organization to support the business objectives, not get in the way. My clients are geniuses at what they do, the best in their fields. I help them create the organizational genius they need to accelerate their ability to reach their vision smoothly and sustainably.

We Develop Accountable Leadership Throughout the Organization

It is not just important—it is actually essential—for every individual in your organization to take responsibility for the success of the business by performing their part with excellence even as they support the success of others.

I offer leadership development programs and coaching to create a culture of accountability and responsiveness, with the end goal of breakthrough business results that are sustainable.

We Create Urgent Business Transformations

The pace of the world means most businesses don't have the luxury of time to make necessary changes. My clients call me when they need to merge departments or organizations, accomplish a key strategic objective on a tight timeframe, get a newly configured leadership team up and functioning at peak efficiency, or any of uncountable other situations in which rapid transformation of the entire business is essential. I have a proven, structured approach that delivers measurable results in three to six months.

We Produce Rapid Team Results

Got a team that needs to hit a number, accomplish an objective, navigate a change or turn around their performance? I offer programs that provide quantifiable changes in team relationships, team execution, and deliverables that ensure meeting reasonable business expectations within six months.

All these programs are built upon a robust accountability system that establishes, measures, and tracks new team standards. We will accomplish in six months what others wish they could accomplish in two years!

To explore how these and other Think Business Growth powered by IMPAQ programs could facilitate growth in your organization, email sharon@thinkbusinessgrowth.com.

Acknowledgments

Many teachers have contributed to my journey and the formation and completion of this book.

Mark Samuel, you changed my life and work by opening up a new world of thinking and action that makes a real and significant difference in the experience and outcomes and lives of our clients.

Annie Hyman Pratt, your down-to-earth wisdom has provided alternate perspectives and helped me believe in myself.

Kamin Bell Samuel, your generous and loving support has helped me get unstuck and find my way back to who I am on more than one occasion.

David Rodgers, Jane Grossman, Barbara Schindler, Heather McGonigal, Anthony Escamillo—and the rest of the IMPAQ global team—you all have provided open-hearted support and immeasurably deepened my understanding of IMPAQ thinking.

Ronen Gafni, creator of the FreshBiz business simulation game, I am so grateful for this brilliant tool and for your ongoing support (along with that of Simcha Gluck and Yosef Funke) that has made it possible for me to transform the way my clients see their businesses, their opportunities, their blindspots, and their ability to create meaningful change in just one play.

Thanks to Henry DeVries, my publisher and developmental editor, along with Devin DeVries, Vikki DeVries, Denise Montgomery,

Joni McPherson, and the rest of the gang at Indie Books International. Massive thanks for including me in your extended family. I'm so grateful to you for doing all the parts of this project that I had no idea how to accomplish.

Deep gratitude and admiration to Moira Schwartz of The Thinking Eye for the cover concept for this book, for branding my business, and for your generous, insightful, design thinking, support, and friendship.

Dale Aviza, you gave me great suggestions to make this read better, and great support to let me know I was on the right track.

My wonderful clients and others whose stories fill these pages: you have transformed me, even as you have trusted me to facilitate your transformations.

Two people who do not even know me, but without whose work this would never have happened are Byron Katie and Esther Hicks. You have inspired me, guided me, and kept me on track, especially during times of great despair. When nothing else helped, you did.

My supportive husband and life partner, Michael Leventhal: You've taught me so much about laughter and fun and loving support, even in the face of great difficulty. Thank you for your grace in accepting me as I am, especially when I am distracted and obsessed with new ideas and projects. And thank you for the reads, re-reads and invaluable insights.

Ariel Leventhal, you have taught me to find love, strength, and compassion—and to persevere and never give up hope.

Last, and most of all, there are not enough words for the enormous appreciation I feel for my brilliant, creative son and writing advisor, Noah Leventhal. You have been intimately involved in this project, have read every word over and over again, provided sage advice and meaningful encouragement. You are wise well beyond your years, Clafouti.

About the Author

After getting to know the hidden game intimately as a leader in the advertising business for twenty-five years, Sharon Rich has dedicated the past decade to transforming business performance by making the invisible visible—facilitating business leaders in bringing their organizations' hidden games out onto the table, where they can rewrite the rules, enter into new conscious agreements, and eliminate the automatic assumptions that get in the way of executing effectively.

Sharon works with businesses that are navigating growth and change in industries that include health care, bioscience, technology, manufacturing, media, professional/creative services, and nonprofits. Sharon is based in Los Angeles. In her free time (along with her husband and two grown children) she plays with self-discovery, writing, painting, cooking, tarot, animals, and travel.

To contact Sharon for more information on her leadership development and team-building programs, please email her at sharon@thinkbusinessgrowth.com.

Works Cited

Barth, John. *Chimera*. London: Deutsch, 1974.

Boushey, Heather, and Sarah Jane Glynn. "There Are Significant Business Costs to Replacing Employees." Center for American Progress website. https://www.americanprogress.org/wp-content/uploads/2012/11/CostofTurnover.pdf.

Bower, Marvin. *The Will to Manage; Corporate Success through Programmed Management*. New York: McGraw-Hill, 1966.

Boyce, Anthony S., Levi R. G. Nieminen, Michael A. Gillespie, Ann Marie Ryan, and Daniel R. Denison. "Which Comes First, Organizational Culture or Performance? A Longitudinal Study of Causal Priority with Automobile Dealerships." *Journal of Organizational Behavior*. January 15, 2015.

Catmull, Ed. *Creativity, Inc.: Overcoming the Unseen Forces that Stand in the Way of True Inspiration*. Random House, 2014.

Covey, Stephen R. *The 7 Habits of Highly Effective People: Personal Workbook*. London: Simon & Schuster, 2005.

Dynamic Signal. "Employee Productivity Statistics: Every Stat You Need to Know." Accessed September 06, 2017. http://dynamicsignal. com/2017/04/21/employee-productivity-statistics-every-stat-need-know/.

Dweck, Carol S. *Mindset: The New Psychology of Success*. New York: Ballantine Books, 2008.

Edmondson, Amy. "Building a Psychologically Safe Workplace," talk given at TEDxHGSE May 4, 2014. http://www.youtube.com/watch?v=LhoLuui9gX8.

Fournies, Ferdinand F. *Why Employees Don't Do What They're Supposed to Do...and What to Do About It*. New York: McGraw-Hill, 2007.

Friedersdorf, Conor. "America Has a Black-Market Problem, Not a Drug Problem." *The Atlantic*. March 17, 2014. https://www.theatlantic. com/politics/archive/2014/03/america-has-a-black-market-problem-not-a-drug-problem/284447/, referencing an Associated Press quote by General John F. Kelly, testifying before the Senate Armed Services Committee.

Gallup, Inc. 2017 report "State of the American Workplace." Gallup. com. http://www.gallup.com/reports/199961/state-american-work-place-report-2017.aspx.

Gilsinan, Kathy. "The Geography of Terrorism." *The Atlantic*. November 18, 2014. https://www.theatlantic.com/international/archive/2014/11/the-geography-of-terrorism/382915/, referencing the "Global Terrorism Index 2014" report by The Institute for Economics and Peace. http://visionofhumanity.org/app/uploads/2017/04/Global-Terrorism-Index-Report-2014.pdf.

Jordan, Michael (script from 1997 Nike commercial) https://www.cbsnews.com/pictures/celebs-who-went-from-failures-to-success-stories/8/. Accessed September 20, 2017.

Katie, Byron. *Loving What Is: Four Questions That Can Change Your Life*. New York: Crown Publishing, 2002.

Leinwand, Paul and Cesare Mainardi. "Stop Chasing Too Many Priorities." *Harvard Business Review*, April 14, 2011. https://hbr.org/2011/04/stop-chasing-too-many-prioriti.

Maxfield, David, and Joseph Grenny. "Culture 2.0: Leveraging Culture for Breakthrough Results." White paper, VitalSmarts. https://www.vitalsmarts.com/resource-center/.

Masters, Brooke. "Rise of a Headhunter," *Financial Times*, March 30, 2009. https://www.ft.com/content/19975256-1af2-11de-8aa3-0000779fd2ac.

Murray, Christopher J.L. and Marie Ng. "Nearly One-Third of the World's Population is Obese or Overweight, New Data Shows." Institute for Health Metrics and Evaluation, May 2014.

Samuel, Mark. *Creating the Accountable Organization: A Practical Guide to Performance Execution*. Katonah, NY: Xephor Press, 2006.

Samuel, Mark. *Making Yourself Indispensable: The Power of Personal Accountability*. New York: Portfolio/Penguin, 2012.

Savov, Vlad. "BlackBerry's Success Led to Its Failure." The Verge. September 30, 2016. http://www.theverge.com/2016/9/30/13119924/blackberry-failure-success.

Seeger, M.W. and R. R. Ulmer. "Explaining Enron: Communication and Responsible Leadership." *Management Communication Quarterly*. (1) 2003. http://www.instituteforpr.org/explaining-enron-communication-and-responsible-leadership/.

Seppala, Emma, and Kim Cameron. "Proof That Positive Work Cultures Are More Productive." *Harvard Business Review*. May 08, 2017. https://hbr.org/2015/12/proof-that-positive-work-cultures-are-more-productive.

Stahl, Ashley. "Here's What Burnout Costs You." *Forbes*. April 16, 2016.

https://www.forbes.com/sites/ashleystahl/2016/03/04/heres-what-burnout-costs-you/#2ce14624e054.

The Engagement Institute. "DNA of Engagement: How Organizations Can Foster Employee Ownership of Engagement." https://www.conference-board.org/dna-engagement2017/

Work Institute "2017 Retention Report—Trends, Reasons & Recommendations." info.workinstitute.com.

Ziglar, Zig and Mayton, Al. *See You at the Top*. Gretna, Louisiana. Pelican Publishing Company, 2012.

Made in the USA
Columbia, SC
06 February 2018